Mind Maps

How to Improve Memory, Write Smarter, Plan Better, Think Faster, and Make More Money

John S. Rhodes

Published by JJ Fast Publishing LLC

Mind Maps

How to Improve Memory, Write Smarter, Plan Better, Think Faster, and Make More Money

Table of Contents

Introduction

Welcome to *Mind Maps and Mind Mapping*. By reading the following material, you will learn you will learn how you can become more focused as well as how you can solve your problems better, faster, and quicker.

You are also going to be learning how to be more creative and how to make more money. In fact, there is a plethora of things that you can accomplish by learning to mind map effectively. You will soon discover why using a mind map can really help you to expand your thinking and how you can improve your quality of life as a result.

The information to follow is divided into twelve chapters. The information therein is broken down as follows:

Chapter 1

The first chapter will define what mind mapping is and how it works. You will also be introduced to some facts and figures about mind mapping that most people have never been exposed to. The history of mind mapping will be reviewed here as well. Some of the greatest minds in history used mind mapping as a means of contemplating their ideas and so can you.

Chapter 2

Chapter 2 is divided into four major sections. The first section covers the various elements of a mind map. The differences between hand drawn and computerized mind maps will be covered in the second section and different ways to put together mind maps will be covered in the third. Finally, the difference between mind maps and mapping will be explained.

Chapter 3

In Chapter 3 you will learn the correct way to make a mind map and why this is important to know. This chapter contains very basic and simple information, but it establishes the foundation for the rest of the training.

Chapter 4

Chapter 4 will go into great detail about how mind maps can help you. You will also be introduced to a concise learning method that you can start to apply right away. This chapter will also help you to identify your learning strategy as well as help you to develop a personal learning plan. Once your learning strategy is deciphered and you develop a learning plan, you can begin to apply it immediately. This will help you in your occupation, business, and even aspects of your personal life.

Chapter 5

Chapter 5 will cover mind maps and learning. 'Learning How to Learn' in relation to mind maps will also be discussed.

Chapter 6

The sixth chapter will explain why mind maps will help you to think smarter. You will also learn the advantages of using mind maps as well as the disadvantages. There are some pitfalls to be wary of, but once you know what they are you shouldn't have any trouble.

Chapter 7

Chapter 7 is a very important chapter. That is why it is broken down into 6 different sections. In the first you will learn how mind mapping encourages creativity. You will also learn about different types of learners and discover what this means for you. The third section will inform you of how you can solve problems using mind maps. Visually powerful tips and tricks will also be provided within this chapter. Finally, you will learn how mind maps can help you to improve learning and memory and help you to overcome procrastination as well as any mental blocks or time blocks that you may have.

Chapter 8

Chapter 8 centers on what you can use mind maps for. A number of different tools, processes, techniques, and systems will be demonstrated which you will find very helpful to use. This is a very hands-on segment of the training.

Chapter 9

There are some shocking ways in which you can use mind maps, which will be covered in Chapter 9. Here you will learn some advanced techniques for using mind maps. This is a very fun and informative chapter.

Chapter 10

In Chapter 10 you will learn how mind maps can make your life better. In other words, you will learn how to use them in a general way to make things better for yourself. You will be surprised at how many possibilities there really are.

Chapter 11

Chapter 11 contains a number different sections through which you will be taught some advanced tips and tricks for using mind maps. For instance, you will learn how you can make your mind maps more appealing as well as how to make them simple and easy to use for yourself and others. You will learn some creative ways to add to your mind maps as well. Finally, you will learn some creative ways to make your mind maps that will help you better express yourself. This chapter will contain some great mind map examples. You will also learn techniques on how to model after the ones that appeal to you. Finally you will learn how to re-do your mind maps in order to get the most value out of them.

Chapter 12

The twelfth chapter is the concluding chapter. This chapter will reiterate the things that you have learned throughout the training. It is where all of these ideas will be brought together as well as where you will learn how to put what you have learned into action.

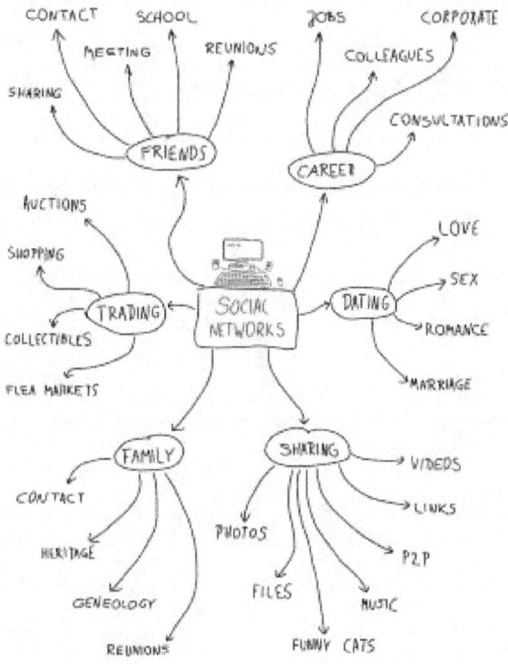

Chapter 1

Mind maps have been used by some of the greatest minds in history for centuries. Learning to use mind maps on a regular basis can vastly improve various capacities in your life and your business. Therefore, it is well worth your time to learn to create mind maps and use them effectively.

What is Mind Mapping?

Mind Mapping can be seen as act of identifying and naming our thoughts and ideas. In some cases this even includes our emotions as well. Once identified, you can arrange them in hierarchical classification. This is an interesting idea because they appear to be non-hierarchal, but they are actually arranged in a hierarchy form, which can be quite useful.

To make a mind map, you begin with a central topic, and then you move outward towards related topics. From those topics you can progress further into other related subtopics. Sometimes there are relationships between the subtopics, so you will find them cross referencing each other. Sometimes you will find these subcategories looping back into one another in a way that this is similar to how flow charts work. This ultimately allows you to hieratically arrange your content, but in such a way that you are able to better visualize it.

Mind maps help you to visually take in the ordering and classification of information, whether it is facts, data, or ideas that you are trying to break apart. A great way to think about a mind map is to think of it as a planetary system, the sun being the central point which is being orbited by planets. Each planet is also being orbited by its own moon. This quick visualization allows you to think about the information in a three-dimensional formation.

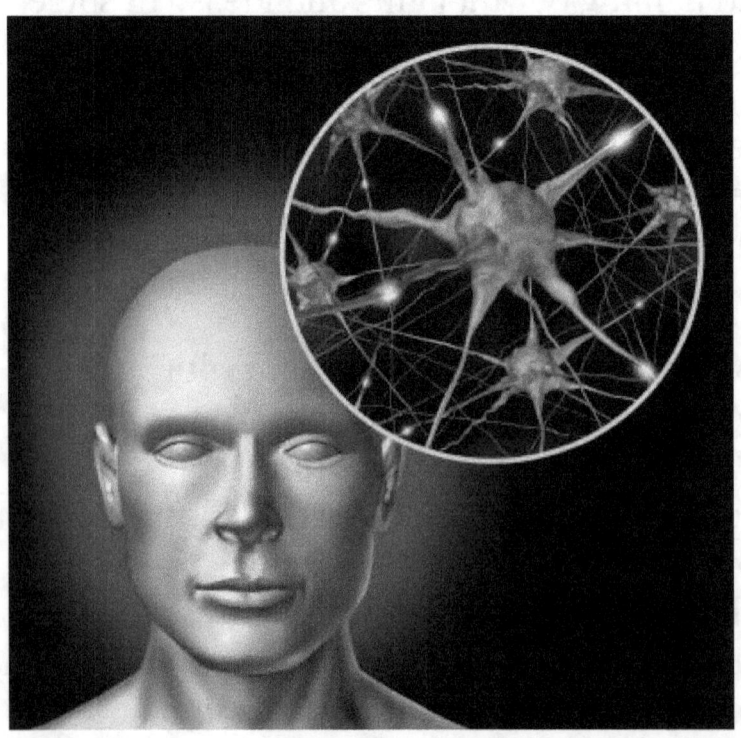

One thing that is interesting about mind maps is that they are very much aligned with what you would see if you could look into someone's mind. The brain works in a similar fashion where one thought or memory is connected to another in a systematic system such as this. For example, if you were to see a clip of a superman movie that you saw as a child, you might connect that memory with a toy that you were playing with at the time you saw that, and because of this memory you are able to recall the name of the company that made that toy. Do you see? Our minds are programmed to work by relating information, which is probably why mind maps work so well.

If you look at the physiology of the human brain, you would see the center of the nerve cell, which branches out to dendrites and axons and so forth. In fact, this physiological system has actually served as the inspiration for many modern mind maps. The mind maps that we see nowadays are therefore reflective of this and other natural systems. Virtually all mind maps are very visual. The topics and subtopics are connected by lines. This creates a flow of information and visually shows the relationship between topics.

You have to realize that mind maps and mind mapping are not the same. The act of mind mapping is a creative act which can help you organize your thoughts and plan ahead. The act of mind mapping can help radically improve your memory and improve efficiency in a profound way. Mind maps are the end result of mind mapping.

The History of Mind Mapping

The act of mind mapping can actually be traced back to the 3rd century BC. The Ancient Greeks were the first known to use mind mapping for intellectual purposes. In fact, the technical term to describe mind mapping, *taxonomy*, is Greek. There are even references to mind mapping and taxonomies in the Bible. For instance, Adam naming the animals represents a type of taxonomy.

This type of taxonomic classification and organization of information is indeed a certain kind of mind map. The concept of mind mapping is a world-wide phenomenon. Mind maps have been found to have come out of Ancient Greece; they were in use all over Europe as well as in Asia. Mind maps have been found to be interconnected with various religions, the emergence of science, and the advancements of agriculture. Think of a family tree. A family tree is not exactly the same as a mind map, but conceptually they are very similar.

In the past, mind maps were generally drawn out by hand. People would often use circles, triangles, and other various shapes to represent the different tiers of information. Arrows and plane lines were, and still are, often used. These very plain symbols were used to collect, organize, and simplify complex information into a visual representation, or more specifically a mind map.

Over the centuries, mind maps have allowed people to better understand and recall information. As humans, we are very good at memorizing certain types of information, especially visual information. Nowadays, because of our technical advancements, putting together a mind map is incredibly easy. Today there are many mind mapping computer programs available, many of which you can get for free.

Mind maps will continue to evolve. As humans learn and advance intellectually, mind maps have become increasingly useful. Mind maps are great for organizing numbers, letters, words, ideas, concepts, and so on, so they are unlikely to go away any time soon. Mind maps are so visual in nature that they allow people who are visual thinkers to much better comprehend the material at hand as well as retain that information. Mind maps are also helpful to people who learn best through audible or drafted information as well since they help people to reinforce what they have learned.

Great Mind Mappers in History

Some of the smartest and most efficient people in history used mind maps regularly. This includes:

Porphyry of Tyros – This philosopher was one of the first known to use mind mapping in his teaching. This brings up a good point. If you are a teacher who is having a hard time getting certain things across to your students, try using a mind map. Porphyry of Tyros probably would have told you the same. He found that he could teach others a lot of information in a much quicker manner by using this tool.

Leonardo Da Vinci – This well known historical figure lived his life in a very efficient manner. He was known to be a painter, inventor, engineer, mathematician, writer, musician, architect, botanist, geologist, sculptor, anatomist, and much more. Da Vinci used mind maps for note taking. Primarily, he used these notes for his own personal advancements.

Instead of using mind maps to communicate concepts and ideas, he collected, organized, and used the information he gathered from their use. Obviously, this allowed Da Vinci to accomplish a lot in his lifetime, which is no surprise. Mind mapping allows us to more quickly get our minds around various concepts. It also allows people to break down content and reorganize information in a number of different ways for a number of different uses.

Albert Einstein – One of the most phenomenal, if not the most phenomenal, minds of the 20th century, Albert Einstein was an avid user of mind maps. He rejected many types of linear, numerical, and even verbal and created ways of thinking. He used mind maps in many unconventional was and he used mind maps to generate unconventional ways of thinking. According to him, this is part of where his creative genius came from.

Much like Leonardo Da Vinci, and Galileo before him, Einstein believed that these types of tools are very useful in expanding the way that we view the world. He believed that these types of tools were more important in capturing our imagination than almost every other type of tool. They also allow us to visually explain things to other people in a way that is very simple to understand. When we have content that is organized and structured it is much easier to understand ourselves and to teach to other people. In fact, it pushes and even forces clarity in thinking.

Specifically, Einstein said "Imagination is more important than knowledge because imagination is unlimited." Not only do mind-maps help you to unfold your imaginative ideas, but they help you to bottle them in such a way that you can understand it, spread it, teach it, share it, and use it. They also allow us to expand upon our thought processes so that we accomplish more.

Dr. Allan Collins — Dr. Collins is an American cognitive psychologist. He is known as one of the fathers of modern mind mapping. In fact, some people would say that he is the father of modern mind mapping because of his extensive commitment to publishing research about creativity, graphical thinking and learning, and so forth. Graphical thinking is thinking that is both visual and structured. This visual structure does not have to be artistic, although it is helpful when it is. According to Dr. Collins, graphical thinking can help us to push forward in creating greater technologies, producing better goods and services, and bringing about mathematical breakthroughs.

Dr. Richard Feynman — Dr. Feynman was an American Nobel Prize winning physicist. At a young age he realized that imagination, creativity, visualization, and the like were the most essential in bringing about breakthroughs. This is true. Working with mind maps can help people to eliminate problems and detonate ideas. One thing that is distinctive about mind maps is that they allow for more play than other tools. Mind maps are very flexible and because they are so visual you can play around with them more and use them in a very game-like fashion.

Tony Buzan – Educational consultant and modern English author, Tony Buzan, is an avid advocate for mind mapping. His belief is that even literate and well-educated individuals are restricted because that you are unable to use many of the conceptual thinking tools that are available, including mind maps.

There are many other famous, highly-talented, very creative, and vastly efficient characters in history that used mind maps on a regular basis, such as Darwin and Beethoven. Many great historical figures also shared the same views about using mind maps as some of the most credible scientists of the modern day. The creative aspects of mind mapping are often what are pointed out to be the most important by these highly intelligent individuals.

Facts & Figures about Mind Mapping

Many people do not know that Boeing Aircraft was actually created from a mind map. It is now one of the largest global manufacturers as well as one of the largest aerospace and defense contractors in the world. Even more interesting is that mind map that was use to craft Boeing was a shocking 25 feet long.

Mind mapping has been used for a long time. Even many of the ancient mind maps and others which have been around for quite some time remain in use to this day. As you can tell from the information above, mind maps continue to be very useful in the modern era and that is not likely to change anytime soon.

Chapter 2

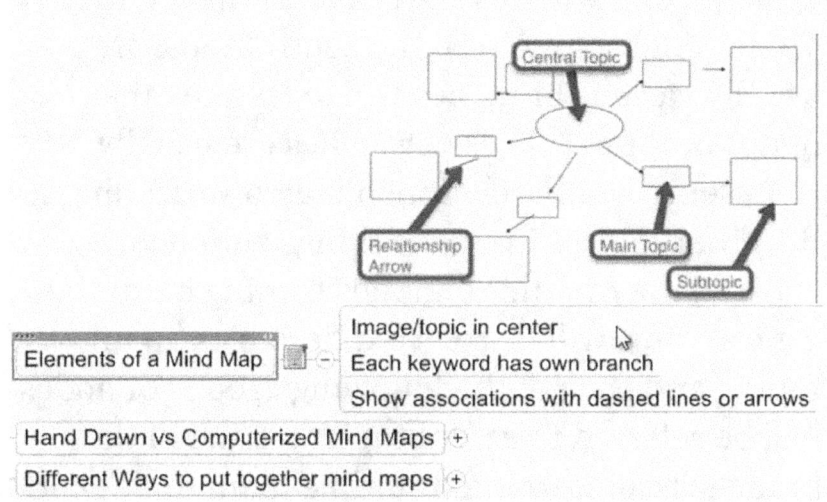

This chapter will explain the different elements of a mind map as well as different techniques and ways of putting one together. This will draw out some of the most basic ideas surrounding the purposes of mind maps and hopefully give you some idea on how to create your own mind maps in the future. The distinctions between mind maps and mind mapping will be made clear as well.

Elements of a Mind Map

The elements of a mind map are actually quite simple. There is always a core central node which depicts and image, a topic, or a central idea. Here it will be referred to as the 'Central Topic'. Stemming from the central topic are usually various branches which lead to other nodes or topics. These branches are usually represented with 'relationship arrows' leading to the other topics. To make things simple to explain, the first tier of nodes coming off of the central topic will be referred herein as 'main topics' and each of the following groups of nodes will be referred to as 'subtopics'. Each of these branches can lead into multiple main topics and subtopics. Furthermore, there is never more than one central topic, as this would call for the creation of another mind map.

There are relationships between the central topic and each of the main topics, just like there are relationships between each of the main topics and the following sub-topics. All of the main topics, in essence, should define the main topic. In other words, if you added them together, each of the main topics should describe the central topic in full. At the very least, the main topics should be put together in such a way that you would be able to tell what the central topic is just by reading the main topics. The same can be said about subtopics in relation to main topics.

Things that are closely related should be clustered together under a main topic. So, you might have multiple subtopics that make up a main topic. A very real-world example will be used to demonstrate this:

Walt Disney used a variety of mind maps to communicate his ideas to others. So, say for example that he was trying to communicate his vision for Disney. Therefore, 'Disney' would be the central topic, and the main topics branching out from there would be 'Disneyland', 'Disney TV', and 'Merchandising'. Branched from the 'Disneyland' main topic would be a cluster of subtopics which would include 'Frontier Land', 'Adventure Land', and 'Tomorrow Land'.

It is obvious how this would work great for planning purposes. This is how Walt was able to oversee everything from books, comic books, and other publications, to the rest of his merchandise, to the theme parks, to the licensing, to the music, to the movies, etc. By using mind maps he was able to oversee a very complex system in a much simpler manner, which allowed his business to become one of the most successful in the world.

Hand-Drawn vs. Computerized Mind Maps

You don't need to use a sophisticated computer program to create a mind map. You can draw one out very quickly on a standard sheet of paper. Obviously, it is much quicker, easier, and cheaper to make your mind maps in this manner. On the other hand, there has been an explosion in the number of computerized mind mapping tools available because they have been found to be so useful.

Computerized mind maps offer more flexibility because you can drag and drop different topics and subtopics and reorganize them as much as you wish. They are also very easy to color code. This allows you to create more than one relationship between the topics and subtopics; this helps you to simplify very complex systems in a clear, easily recognizable manner.

Drawing is not a requirement of either type, but mind map programs make it easier to use pictures to symbolize different topics or points in the mind map. In fact, there is often a plethora of images, illustrations, and graphics that you can utilize. There are also different flowchart-type images that you can use in expressing the relationships between the topics clearly.

If you need a flow chart to carry around, you have the ability to print these out. Therefore, you have both the option of having a digital copy available or you can have a physical copy that you can store or keep on hand to use. That means that if you are on the run to somewhere and won't have access to your computer, you can print your mind maps out and use them while you are gone. On the other hand, you have a digital copy that you can email to yourself and then you can access it from any computer anywhere.

Most likely, if you start to use mind maps, you will begin sketching them out on paper as you go through your day. However, as you begin using mind mapping software, you will probably gravitate towards your computer more and more since you can make much clearer and creative forms mind maps within this software. Of course, this all will have to do with how you are using your mind maps to begin with as well as what they are being created for.

Different Ways to Put Together Mind Maps

One reason mind maps are so great to use is that they are extremely flexible and you can use them in a great number of different ways. There are lots of different ways that you can put together a mind map. To get you started, there are three basic approaches that you can begin using immediately:

Open & Get Cracking — All you do to get started with this method is put your central topic on the paper, draw a few lines going out to main topics, and then start letting your ideas flow, using any tools that you have at your disposal to build onto it. This is a very basic method, where you begin with an idea and you start building from the ground up. This is one of the best ways to use a mind map to come up with ideas.

Take Notes & Then Mind Map — Another approach is to begin taking notes and gathering all the information that you need, and then formulate a mind map out of the information in the notes, categorizing the information as you do so. Obviously, this method is a little bit more advanced than the previous one. This would work best for planning things out and communicating your ideas.

Different Levels of Involvement — This method involve the use and reuse of information. It is best to use when there are different levels of involvement based on different needs. When you use this approach, you may use different templates that are available, or add to old mind maps. This will allow you to take the information that is already there and edit it and adjust it in various ways.

The previous techniques allow you to learn the content better and reclassify the information based on new ideas and concepts. You may even have two or more mind maps open at the same time in order to add and combine the best information from the two. It is best to use a computerized program for this type of mind mapping, but you don't have to.

The Difference between Mind Maps & Mind Mapping

There is a big difference between mind maps and mind mapping that is important to recognize. Mind maps are the actual output. They are the end result of the mind mapping process. Mind maps are generally made up of bits of content such as bits of codes, bits of concepts, or bits of data. These bits of content have been gathered up, organized, and arranged into a hierarchy within the mind map. These bits of content can be in the form of words, numbers, or images. Often, simple shapes or colors will be used to illustrate their relationship.

Not only do you get a better idea of what you are trying to put together by using a mind map, but others do too. With all of your information being broken up in this way, people are usually able to understand the entire concept in a few seconds or minutes. In other words, this is a tremendously effective way to communicate ideas.

Mind-mapping, on the other hand, is a creative process. This process allows you to organize your thoughts or expand upon them better, because you are breaking your ideas apart in such a clear manner. It also makes it easier to understand the relationships between the various elements being recognized. The point of the mind-mapping process is to organize information and/or come up with ideas. You can create a mind map for your own personal use, or you can use it to share your ideas or existing data with others in a very simple way.

You can also use mind maps to collaborate with each other. For example, you might start a computerized mind map and email it to a business partner so that they can add to it and send it back to you. For complex systems, this can save a lot of time and energy because you don't have to worry about discussing every point of what you are working on together. In fact, everything can be worked and re-worked without anyone having to say a word.

The act of mind mapping helps you to retain information. In other words, going through the process of mind mapping will help you to understand and take in the information more easily. Also, because the information is put together visually, and in little bits, it is easy to take it in. Finally, the chunking of the bits of information makes it easy to remember, since chunking is a mnemonic device.

Mind-mapping is one of the most effective ways to create and expand on your ideas. In other words, the mind mapping process helps new ideas to manifest. The process also helps you to work through your thoughts and emotions, making them tangible and useable. Putting a 'pen to paper' in this way not only helps you to retain the information in your memory, but documents it as well.

To reiterate, mind mapping is the actual act of creating and organizing ideas and data. A mind map is the final output of this process. So, one is the result and one is the activity that yields the result. This is an important distinction to understand before moving forward. They both have their purposes, and they both allow you to learn and create in unique ways. The following chapters will show you how this is done.

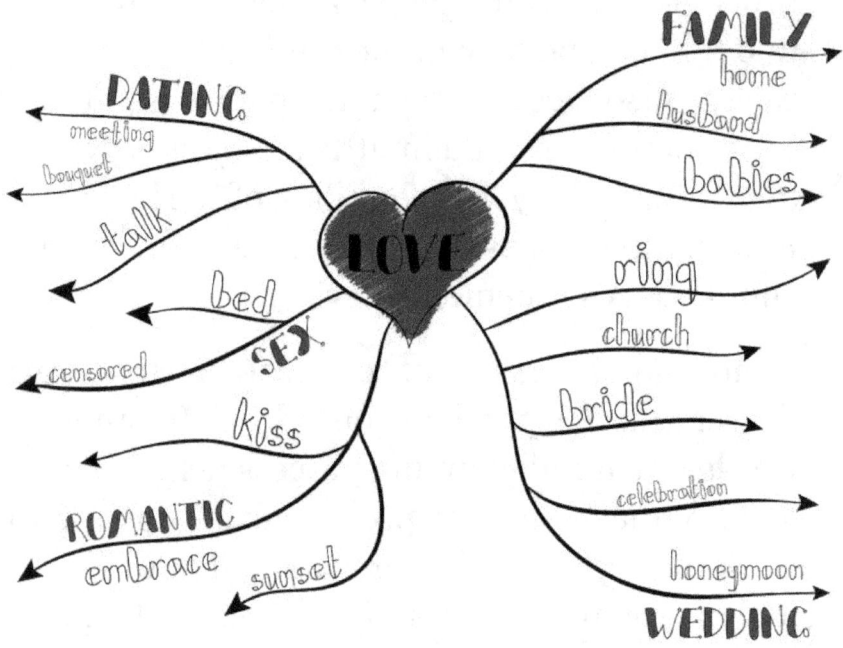

Chapter 3

Singular Keywords

Length of the branch should be the same as the word

Main topic lines are thicker than subtopic

Group similar items together

This chapter outlines the correct way to make a mind map. There are many different ways to create mind maps and many different ways to use them. In fact, a plethora of different rules have been established for putting them together. Mind maps do not have to be done the same way every single time. They are versatile by nature. However, there are some things that you must do in order to get the most value out of them.

When you are creating a mind map, it is best to use singular keywords. This means that you want to use singular concepts and singular ideas, instead of trying to fit multiple ideas into one topic or sub-topic. You want to break these ideas or pieces into the smallest form possible so that your sub-topics can cleanly break off of that one topic with no confusion. You are really going after one single concept, data point, or idea.

When you create a main topic, it should so fully encapsulate that main idea in such a way that the supporting subtopics easily relate to the main keyword. For example, in most cases you wouldn't want to use something like 'Fruits & Vegetables' for your main keyword. Instead, you would want to use the keyword 'Fruit' and followed with subtopics like 'Banana', 'Apple', 'Orange', etc. That allows you to look at that specific main topic of fruit and clearly understand everything that is associated with that main topic of 'Fruit'. In this case, everything that follows should be a type of fruit.

Usually when you see subtopics coming off of a topic, the relationship is one to where the main idea carries over. There is transference of the idea, or main concept, downward. So, with the main topic being 'Fruit' and 'Apple' being a subtopic, you know that 'Apple' is a type of fruit. It is that clear relation that gives the hierarchy that was created so much power. That is why you go after singular keywords.

Now, a less specific way to think about this is that the length of the branch should be the same as the word. Subtopics should not be paragraphs and paragraphs of content. At most it should be a short sentence, made up of just a few words. The same thing applies to main topics and the central topic. You don't want a giant mind map that is loaded with words. You want to be as concise as possible. This length requirement isn't really a requirement at all, just a guideline that should be followed.

Main topic lines can be thicker than subtopic lines. This symbolically shows that the main topics are more powerful or more closely related to the central topic. This visual representation gives you a lot of information at a glance. The same guideline applies to arrows. By the way, if there are arrows used, this symbolically states 'it's of this kind', 'it's related to', or 'the information flows in that direction'. So, sometimes you will see arrows in a mind map, and sometimes you won't because arrows refer to the information flow.

The final guideline is that you must group like items together. You can do this in a variety of ways. You can use similar shapes or similar colors to group information. Just the fact that you have a central topic leading to a main topic which in turn leads into subtopics makes a statement. You are saying that this information is related, which is essentially the whole point of grouping in a mind map.

The way that the information is presented visually tells you an awful lot, even at a glance. You can move these topics and subtopics around at any time to re-think or re-organize these topics as needed to show that one 'holds more weight' than another and so on. This is especially easy to do when using software.

These guidelines were meant to help you understand the basic rules for creating mind maps and the reasons for each. Of course, you can break these rules at any time. You can organize the information in any way that helps you best. However, knowing these rules can help you to communicate to yourself and others more effectively.

Chapter 4

In this chapter you will learn how mind maps can help you. A concise learning method will be presented to you. You will also have the chance to identify what your learning strategy should be and be able to reflect upon yourself the mind mapping process. Finally, you will be led through the process of designing a personal learning plan of your own.

How Can Mind Maps Help You?

Perhaps the most important thing about mind maps is that they will allow you to understand a topic in its entirety. You are also able to view the most critical elements of that topic at a glance. Whether on a screen or on a piece of paper you can identify what you should be thinking about and what it is that you are trying to plan out. This allows you to brainstorm very quickly and at a deeper level than most other methods would allow you to do.

Whatever problem you are trying to solve or whatever information you are trying to understand can be very easily grasped when you are using a mind map. This is why mind maps make great learning devices and are great for communicating with or teaching others as well. Since mind maps are so visual, it is easy to see how each topic and topic relates to one another by how each topic is categorized or grouped. Most of the time this understanding comes to you at a glance by the way the information is organized.

While you are in the process of creating a mind map, you will find that the act itself will help your ideas to manifest. Essentially, as you are thinking about all of the topics and subtopics, you will be forced to create more subtopics in order to move forward. This, of course, allows you to break apart the problem or the details of the data even further. Eventually, this will provide clarity in your thinking.

The more this information is broken down, the quicker you will be able to understand and grasp it. When you compare this process to other forms of informational communication, such as in a book, manual, or even a picture, you will see how much more quickly the information can be taken in. A mind map allows you to observe a mixture of information in a very quick manner, making it superior to many other forms of data. One of the reasons why mind maps are often so much more efficient is that you can blend both text and images. You can blend the two in any way you need to.

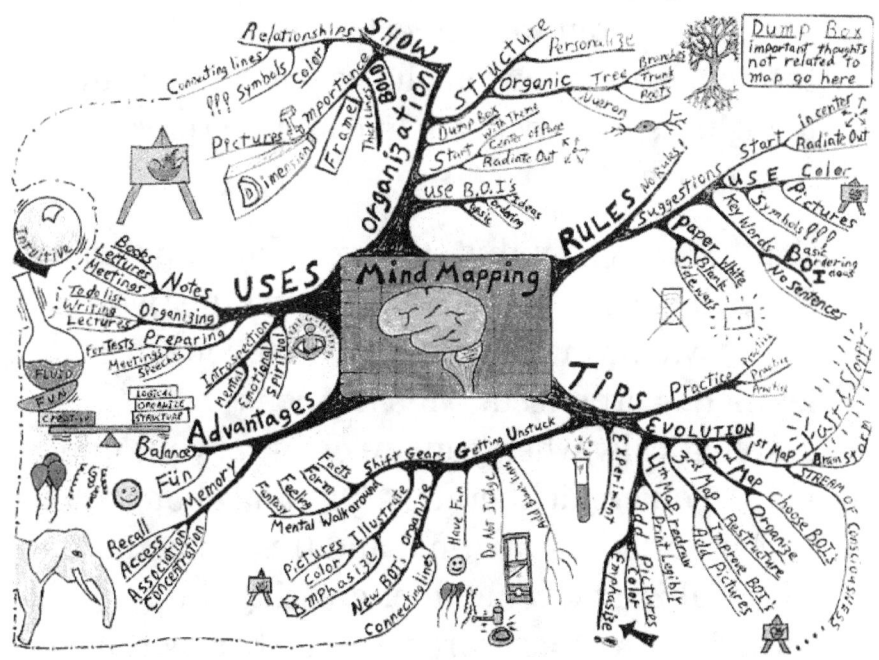

Mind Map created by Charles MacInerney - charles@expandingparadigms.com

Concise Learning Method

The following information was derived from *The Concise Learning Method for 21st Century Students,* which was developed by Professor Tony Krasnic. The steps to this concise learning method are as follows:

Step 1: Preview — The first step is to preview the content by quickly glancing at the materials beforehand.

Step 2: Participate — The second step is to actively participate in a discussion about the material. This will work even if the discussion occurs internally. To do this you could ask yourself questions about the subject. This step begins the engagement which allows you to go from being passive to being active and therefore productive.

Step 3: Process — In this step, you think about and store the memory of the topic. In other words, this is when your memory of what you have learned is produced. This happens automatically when you are creating your mind map. You are deliberately thinking about what you are typing or writing, and this act helps you to visualize and remember creating this material. In other words, remembering the creation of the mind map will help you to remember the material itself.

Step 4: Practice — When using mind maps, you can 'practice' by writing, re-reading, or paraphrasing the material. Reciting the material would also help you to practice. Really, any way of reviewing the material could be considered a 'practice', so feel free to do whatever works best for you. Reviewing information three times has been shown to help people store things to memory.

Step 5: Produce – The next step is to produce, or show that you have retained the knowledge in some way. This can be done by writing a report, taking a test, or just writing out what you have learned from memory. This forces you to not only recognize the information but retrieve it from memory as well.

Memorization is really two different forces at play. First, there is the ability to recognize information, and second is your ability to recall the information. Retrieval of information from memory is a higher skill. It is important that you're not just recognizing it, that you are actually able to retrieve it.

The best way to understand this is through different forms of testing. True & False or Multiple Choice tests would be examples of tests where you are asked to recognize the right answer. An essay exam, on the other hand, would be an example of a test where you would have to retrieve the information about a subject from memory. A short answer test would be an example of this as well. In both circumstance you are being asked to re-create the information.

The more that you create the more you'll remember, but you must be able to recall the information to make it useable. That is why the 'Production' step is what drives everything home. Recalling this information and applying it is really a productive act because you are reproducing (or recreating) the information from memory. Every step in the process is important, however. Each of these 5 steps requires that you:

- Identify key concepts

- Meaningfully organize and connect key concepts

- Think critically

- Ask key questions

You automatically go through each of these steps when you create a mind map. In the process of creating a mind map you are also identifying key concepts, connecting and organizing those concepts, thinking critically about the topic, and asking key questions. Therefore, the act of mind mapping automatically contains the most critical elements of this advanced learning process.

Obviously, following this concise learning method will help you to learn and move forward faster. Using it all the time through the formulation of mind maps will multiply these results exponentially. Tony Krasnic, by the way, is a firm believer in using mind maps to expedite learning.

What's Your Learning Strategy?

Now, shift your mind into thinking about the tactics that you can use to learn faster, memorize better, and become more productive. There are, in fact, a large variety of tactics that you can use. They include:

Word ID – Using this tactic involves breaking words into three parts: the prefix, suffix, and stem. The prefix can be found at the beginning of the word, the suffix can be found at the end, and the stem is of course the core of the word itself. So, take the word 'submarine' for example. The prefix of the word, 'sub' means below and the stem of the word is 'marine', which refers to water. So, by breaking up the word you know that a submarine is something that exists below water. Being able to break up words in this way allows you to better understand and learn content.

This also helps you to teach other people. You can also use a mind map to teach this tactic to people more quickly. For example, if you wanted to teach a child how to find the meaning of more difficult words, you could use a mind map to break words into their component parts.

Self-Questioning – This tactic involves creating questions and then seeking out the information to answer them. If you already have the answers, then you can test yourself by listing the questions to be answered in the mind map, and then trying to recall them on your own.

Visual Imagery – This tactic involves using mental visualization to retain information. For example, if you were going to the store to get bread, oranges, and milk, instead of writing them out a list, you could memorize them by visualizing your trip. So, you would picture yourself going to the produce section and picking out the oranges, then moving onward to the isle where the bread is at, and then moving to the back of the store, grabbing the milk and putting it in your basket. If you do this 'walk through' beforehand, you will have no trouble remembering the items that you need when you get to the store.

This 'walk through' is like creating a movie in your head. Adding details to your 'movie' like thinking of the scenery or adding character will also help you to remember details more clearly as well. For example, imagining yourself putting the milk in the basket in your mental walk-through is probably going to help you remember the milk more than any of the other products. Now, if you were to write these details down in a mind map directly after visualizing yourself doing this, this would reinforce the memory you made, making you far less like to forget.

Inference – The idea here is that you can think about a topic and use logic to draw conclusions. Then, you perform research to see if your conclusions are correct. You can use a mind map to capture the questions, organize them, and then try to answer them on your own. Afterwards you go look up the information to find the real answers. Then, you compare the answers that you found with those within the mind map. You can then add what you learned to the mind map, which would drive the learning process that much more.

Quick Paraphrasing & Summarizing – In this method, you make short statements that define the topic. In other words, when you are learning something, you can capture the information in the form of short sentences to make the information more memorable. You can push this method even further by deriving keywords from those short sentences and then using a mind map to make associations between the keywords. You could even derive these keywords from the information that you're studying, and skip the act of forming the sentences entirely. Making the connections between these keywords will help you to retrieve the information from memory, reinforcing what you have just learned.

Paraphrasing – This tactic involves re-writing the information in your own words. Again, you can reinforce the information by recreating the information by creating a mind map out of what you paraphrased.

Reflect

When you reflect upon a certain aspects in your life, try to relate what it means to you. You can ask yourself what it means to you in relation to work, in terms of the relationships that you have with friends and family, and in the broad sense of yourself. You're always learning, so this means that this reflection would change over time, whether you want it to or not. So, when you experience something new, this gives you the opportunity to revisit a mind map, reflect once more, and revise the material.

Changes may occur in a very short period of time. For example, you may have reflected upon your position at work, but then you have a conversation with a co-worker which changes your whole perception. So, the next time you open up that mind map, it is time to reflect once more. Another example would be going to a training session or conference. When you return, you may have a totally different outlook about the project that your business has taken on. So, at this point, you might pull up the old mind-map that pertains to that project, reflect upon what you thought before, and re-adjust it according to the new outlook that you have.

You don't have to perform this reflection in front of a computer either. You can jot down mind maps on pieces of paper at any point in time. Doing this often can help you reflect upon your life, your goals, and your relationships, allowing you to fix your problems, work towards your goals, and clear your mind on a consistent basis. This would not only help you to constantly relieve stress, but to continuously be working on your goals as well. You can get a lot out of this, especially when you reflect upon what any particular subject means to your life. Take the time to reflect, capture ideas, and grab all the opportunities that you can to keep the right outlook and improve your life.

Design a Personal Learning Plan

The smartest thing that you can do in your life is to have a strategy planned for learning as much as possible. You don't have to write this down, but obviously it is better if you do. Having this strategy planned will allow you to apply the right tactics at the right time. Before you start this process, there are a few personal questions that you should ask yourself. They are:

- Why are you learning what you are learning?

- What is it that you are trying to get out of the learning activity?

- What are you planning to use mind mapping for?

- When should you be using mind mapping to get the results that you want?

You are creating this plan so that you can get the most out mind mapping for your own purposes. You may also be doing so as attempt to train and teach others. This process helps you to learn about yourself and how you learn best, which you can later use to help others as well.

Simply by using mind maps, you can learn about how you learn. You will learn about the type of language that you use, how you group and organize information, and what best helps you to retain information. Mind mapping can help you to reflect upon where you need to improve as well as where your strengths are. You can pick the methods and tools that suit you best and get the most out of your time and effort. Don't try to do it all at once; it is a learning process.

Once you have discovered what your learning style is, you can apply the learning tactics that work best for you when you are mind mapping. Be sure that you use some of the tactics that have been outlined above because they are scientifically proven to work. By learning to use mind maps effectively, you can improve your learning, you can better teach and train others, and improve your own life, relationships, and business.

Chapter 5

One of the best things about mind maps is that they allow you to brainstorm. Brainstorming really is nothing more than sitting down in a relaxed fashion and trying to solve a problem or come up with ideas. You can do this in a group or on your own.

Mind mapping allows you to jot down any ideas that come to mind, no matter how crazy or off the wall. Sometimes the wilder an idea is the better because they tend to spark new ideas and new concepts. So, when working with other, you want to provide encouragement no matter what types of ideas they come up with. Mind mapping will help you to jot down these ideas and the associations between those ideas. Even in a group, this allows you to brainstorm very quickly and very effectively.

When you are done brainstorming, you can go back and rework the ideas that you have come up with. It also allows you to come back and explore these ideas. When you do, you can reorganize the information so that it can be communicable to others or easily understood when you revisit it later. So, while you are brainstorming, don't worry about getting everything organized at first. Just come up with as many ideas as you can and go back and organize them later.

Mind maps allow you to more easily communicate your ideas to others. It also allows you to communicate better with yourself as well. When you have a hard time figuring out a problem, or when you feel overwhelmed, you can simply use a mind map to better break things apart and better understand them.

Since you are using simple words and phrases, you don't have to come up with anything profound when you are using a mind map. This allows things to flow out of your mind more freely. It also allows you to chip away at the problem or break into an idea a little at a time. Just use whatever words or phrases come to mind, and you will naturally come up with new ideas. Mind mapping forces you to break down your thought processes and reorganize them in a way that makes sense. This helps you to better understand things.

Think of an atom. Each one of the keywords, pictures, and ideas are the atoms that make up a molecule. As you add these ideas you are creating something bigger, and when you reorganize these atoms and molecules, you end up with completely new materials. The 'molecule' that you have created may be a small part of something much bigger, but the more you create, the more you'll end up with.

If you use mind maps on a regular basis, you will soon discover that you are able to recall information more easily. This is especially true for the information that you have mapped out. Mind maps are broken down into basic information. So, essentially it is like being given candy in bite-sized chunks. Not only is it easy to take this information in, but by the way it is organized, you can understand the relationship between things at a glance. So, you have an overall understanding after reviewing a mind map for just a moment.

Mind mapping also allows you to better plan out tasks. Say, for example, that you wanted to plan out the chores for the members of your household. Your central topic would be 'Household Chores', the main topics would be the names of each of the family members that you have living in your house, and the subtopics would be a listing of every family member's assigned chores. Do you see how effective that can be?

You could also plan out your week this way by making the central topic 'What to do this week' and the main topics each day of the week. The subtopic would be every task that you needed to accomplish. You could use this mind map as a template and simply readjust the information day by day or as you needed to. This would obviously be helpful because you would have everything planned out and you would be able to review this information at a glance.

What about planning for more complex events such as a wedding? Mind mapping this out could really help you to communicate to others what their role is and what they are responsible for. If you are doing this by computer, this information could be passed along quickly and easily. You could sit with a piece of paper and plan everything out with friends and family, and recreate or reorganize the information by computer as many times as necessary.

Obviously, mind mapping helps you to organize your thoughts and ideas. That is why writers use them so often. As their ideas change or expand, these documents can easily be recreated and reorganized. When the entire story is mapped out this way before it is even written, you can ensure that all the events that you want are included and that they fall into the correct places in your book. This can be applied to any situation where plans, thoughts, and ideas need to be laid out in advance and are likely to change often.

As was touched upon in the previous lessons, mind maps can help you to learn how to learn. They also boost your creativity because the process of mind mapping invites ideas. One of the great things about mind maps is that it displays text but in a very graphic sort of way. In other words, even if there are no images within your mind map, you are getting a very visual representation of what is being outlined. Plus, by reorganizing your topics and subtopics you are able to make connections that you may have never imagined before.

Using a mind map also gets rid of distractions. This is because it provides you with a layout and structure of the information that you would not otherwise get. For example, if you were sitting around thinking of what you needed to pack for your trip, your line of thought might wane towards other things that you need to get done before you leave town. If you were making a mind map, you could throw this in as a thought to remember, but then continue on planning what you were going to pack. Do you see how this can help you to focus in better?

Even if you couldn't draw a stick figure to save your life, you can still create a graphical representation of your content. This is wonderful because it allows people easy ways to share and review information visually, even if they cannot draw these images out themselves. This can be quite empowering. It can spark creativity which you didn't even know that you have, it can allow you to communicate ideas better and faster, and it can allow you to review the information at a glance. Often times this will make the mind map seem more fun and creative, and therefore more effective.

Using a computerized mind map can be especially helpful if you are planning out a book. You can begin outlining it with the table of contents, and then add in tiers of information within each chapter. As you are doing so, you can also add in the illustrations, charts, and graphs in their proper places. This, of course, will allow you to view the layout of your book before you even begin writing.

When you are mind mapping, you will find that the mind map keeps your brain engaged from multiple angles. This is because it is not laid out in a linear fashion like an outline would be. When your brain is engaged like this, it puts you into a transient-like state. It is well-known that when a person is in this state, or in 'the zone' as it is often deemed, this removes mental blocks and both sides of the brain are allowed to work. So, this allows for communication between both sides of the brain which would not normally occur. This also allows the brain to become more creative and more receptive to ideas.

Mind maps are very cool because they allow for, and encourage, both organized and creative thought. The mixture of numbers, text, and images that you can use to express your ideas are unending. Plus, they open your mind up in a way that allows better ideas and concepts to flow in a better way than you would get by any other means. So, when you work on your mind maps, try to become relax, yet engaged so that you are able to come up with the best ideas and solutions possible.

Chapter 6

By now you should have a good grasp on how useful mind maps can be. They are so flexible that you can use them for almost anything. Plus, mind maps help you to open your mind and think smarter as well. There is a theory pertaining to how humans can most optimally think. It is called 'Whole Brain Thinking'. Mind mapping can cause whole brain thinking to occur, which allows you to think smarter, better, and faster.

Basically, what the 'Whole Brain Thinking' theory states is that human beings think in the following four ways:

1. Logical – Focuses on the facts and the bottom line

2. Creative – Sees the big picture and likes to have fun

3. Practical – Provides organization and follow through

4. Relational – Tunes in to his/her own and other's feelings

Some people are more logical, and some are more creative. Some people tend to be more practical, while others tend to rely on their feelings. However, all of us have the ability to think in each of these four different ways, although sometimes we tend to think in one way over another. All of these forms of thinking work simultaneously with one another.

Logical thinking is about focusing on the bottom line. It is the type of thinking that helps us to rationalize things like if a=b and b=c, the 'a' must equal 'c' as well. Creative thinking allows us to see the bigger picture of things. It also is the side of us that allows us to play and have fun.

The relational side to our thinking allows us to tune into our emotions as well as those of others. This also has to do with how we deal with both tangible and intangible things in the world around us. So, through this way of thinking we can relate to various ideas and concepts in very much the same way as we relate to other people. Most importantly, practical thinking allows us to organize and then take action.

One of the reasons why mind maps are so special is that they tap into all of these forms of thought. Mind mapping allows you to see how various concepts and ideas fit together in a logical manner, for example. There is also a very visual element to mind maps which allow you to see 'the entire picture' at a glance, which taps into the creative side to our thinking. In addition to this, mind mapping allows us to formulate ideas and play around with concepts. So, it appeals to our creative side in that way as well.

Our relational thinking is also what allows us to see the relationships between objects and concepts, which has already been established as a vital part of the process of mind mapping. Seeing these relationships helps us to organize our thoughts and expand upon our ideas in a logical way. Relational thinking also applies that as we are mapping things out. A lot of what we write out relates to how we feel about one thing or another as our creative mind is pumping out ideas. Practical reasoning is what drives us to organize the information in a mind map so that we can turn it into a useable form and take action.

As you may realize, all of these forms of thinking work both in concert with one another and to a certain extent are interconnected with one another. Mind mapping allows us to open up each of these forms of thought and allows them to work in greater harmony with one another. All of these lines of thought are tapped into when someone is reviewing the information on a mind map as well, which is one of the reasons why mind maps are so easy to learn from. It allows the whole brain to become engage. In other words, it allows for whole brain thinking.

All of the different pieces of what it is to be human can be represented in a mind map. Mind maps are designed this way. They are designed to be used in all of these different ways so that any type of goal can be accomplished through them. The fact that they are designed to encompass different forms of thinking allows you to think on a much higher scale than you normally would otherwise.

If you have never used a mind map, you should try it out right now. Simply get out a piece of paper, and begin your own journey by experiencing this for yourself. This way you know from experience what a mind map can do for you before moving forward. There is really an infinite amount of ways that this form of planning and deciphering of information can help you to improve upon your business, your relationships, and your life.

So, specifically, what are the advantages to using mind maps? First of all, they are more compatible with the brain than other tools. In other words, the way that mind maps work is very compatible in the way that we think as humans. Humans have a need for balance and organization and mind maps provide us a way of accomplishing this. They appeal to our fun and creative sides as well. Also, the way in which humans solve big problems is to either chip away at them a little at a time or by taking small steps to accomplish big tasks. Mind maps allow us to do all of this by encouraging how we naturally think.

Mind maps also appeal to the senses. This is because you are able to become more engaged with them than you would with most other types of tools. So, they have a way of 'coming to life' even though they are essentially just notes on paper. They also balance the brain and remove any blocks that disallow different parts of our brain to work in balance with one another.

Other advantages of using mind maps over other types of tools are that they clearly show associations, enhance creativity, and make it easier and faster to take and review notes. One of the reasons for this is because mind mapping is a way to record information in creative and visual contexts. For example, you can use various shapes and colors to represent different categories or levels. This allows information to be quickly understood, sometimes even at a glance. This is a fun, creative, and visual type of learning. Any teacher will tell you that the brain is most receptive when information is presented in fun, creative, and visual ways. That is the main reason why mind maps make incredible learning tools.

There are disadvantages to using mind maps as well. For instance, sometimes mind maps cause a person to think in too simplistically. So, sometimes you have to step back and take a bird's eye view of the information to make it make sense. In other words, when you are working with a mind map, sometimes you are working on things at such a small scale that you cannot see the bigger picture.

Another disadvantage to using mind maps is that they sometimes take more time to draw out if you are dealing with a complex problem. Again, this is because with mind maps you begin working at such a small scale. Complex problems, therefore, usually call for more than one mind map or an extensive one, which may not be worth your time and energy. Just think of the one that was created for Boeing Aircraft. It ended up being 25 feet long. In this case, it was well worth it, however.

Finally, some people have trouble learning to use mind maps. There are people who don't feel that they would use it enough to take the time to learn how to do it. That is fine, although most people can pick this up rather easily. When they do, they usually find that it helps them immensely.

Sometimes people just get overwhelmed by the software as well. Although computerized mind mapping programs have their advantages, you don't always need all of these extra features to create an effective mind map. This is especially true if you are only trying to plan or break apart problems for your own personal needs. There is nothing wrong with just scribbling your ideas out on paper to use for your own needs, or creating a mind map on some poster-board in order to share your ideas with everyone else.

At times it really isn't worth the time and effort to use mind maps, especially if there are other tools that work better for your line of work or your style of planning. Mind maps really do hold a lot of advantages over other forms of planning and brainstorming tools, however. In fact, the advantages of using mind maps greatly outweigh the disadvantages in most cases. They truly do help you to think smarter, and help you to communicate smarter with other people too. Furthermore, the final outcome of a mind-mapping session is usually far superior to the outcomes of other similar types of activities.

Mind mapping not only helps you to brainstorm and come up with new ideas quickly, but it opens up your mind so that it works in an optimal way. As you are brainstorming you are recording your ideas. Plus, after you are done, you can go back and edit or reorganize the information as much as you like. Finally, when all of this is done, you have a communicable compilation of facts and ideas that you can use to demonstrate your plans, share ideas, and even teach others with.

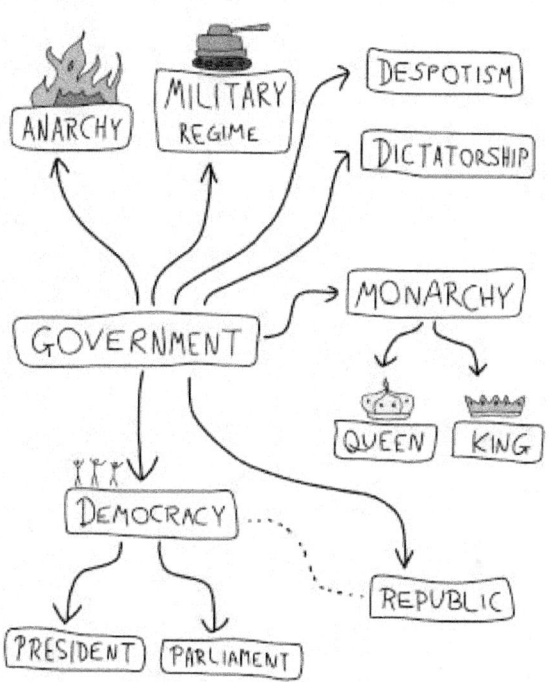

Chapter 7

This chapter focuses on creativity and the different ways in which people learn. You will also learn about the many ways that mind maps can help you to solve problems, learn more, and overcome some of things that are blocking you from achieving your goals. In other words, this information will help you learn how to use mind maps in the most optimal manner.

Mind Maps & Creativity

Mind maps encourage your creativity. This is because, among other things, they help you to avoid linear thinking. Linear thinking is a very limited way of thinking. If you were to take a trip, for example, you may run into situations where you have to think creatively... figure out the right direction to go, what to eat, and where to stay at. On the other hand, if you were to take a drive on a route that you have covered hundreds of times before, there is really no thought process involved. You pretty much do it automatically. This is like linear thinking. Linear thinking is not deep or creative; it is just thinking at your most basic level.

Mind mapping forces you to think in deeper, more diverse, and more creative ways. In other words, mind mapping forces you to open up and look at things in an entirely new manner and open yourself up to new ideas. Even more importantly, it pushes you into coming up with new ideas on your own.

When you are mind mapping, you are able to move around all of your topics and subtopics. As you move the information you will find that a little tiny opening for creativity presents itself. As you continue working, this opening for creativity continues to expand. So, eventually you are putting information into the mind map and extracting out ideas.

One thing that is interesting is that mind mapping allows you to be creative, yet very realistic. When you are first beginning to brainstorm your ideas, it is likely that your mind map will get pretty messy. Naturally, the ideas that we have are not very orderly. For one thing, it is very difficult for humans to group things in their mind ahead of time. Aside from that, the thoughts that we jot down are often incomplete and unstructured. You have to spend time with the material in order for it to become organized.

Having to go to through the process of organizing the material is actually a good thing.

Think of a writer who is writing a story. If she were to jot down ideas for a story on a piece of paper, and then just start writing the story, the details of that story would be more logical and more attuned than when she first wrote them down. However, if she were to write them into a mind map, she may have to go back and reorganize the information to make more sense of it, but this extra step would make her material more detailed and more logical when she finally did write out her story. So, the creative ideas would still be there, but now the information would be set up in a more realistic and detailed manner.

As stated above, mind maps have a way of forcing you to be more creative. This is because the mind map itself is a creative tool. By nature mind maps have a way of hooking into the right side of the brain. In fact, you will probably find yourself tapping into a creative side that you didn't even know that you had. A lot of the mind mapping process is dependent on your own intuition. So, as you are reorganizing the information, brand new ideas naturally manifest.

In many cases you will find that subtopics will suddenly become brand new when you move them from one topic to the next. It is kind of like when you look at something from a different angle, all of the sudden looks totally different. Things tend to seem differently when you collect or gather them together with other chunks of information, just like something suddenly seems small when you place it beside something bigger.

When you move these subtopics around, they have to be reconsidered, which again causes you to become more creative in your thinking. While you are going through this process, you are tapping into your intuition. You then try and figure out what is the right combination according to the gut feeling you have about what is correct or incorrect.

Different Types of Learning

Everyone has a different type of learning style. For the most part, there are watchers, readers, and listeners. Watchers really enjoy videos. That is probably the most optimum way for them to learn. They also learn well from visual elements, such as pictures, images, and more interesting forms of text. Readers take in information best when it is written out. Finally, there are listeners, which take in information best in auditory form.

Mind maps work best for watchers and readers. This, of course, makes sense because the information is presented in a visual manner which includes text. However, it is not like mind maps are not advantageous to listeners as well. Listeners can get a lot out of information out of a mind map, especially when they can look at a mind map as the information within is being explained. They can also benefit from writing the information into a mind map as they are listening to it. So, all three different types of learners can benefit from using mind maps and mind mapping.

Mind Maps Help You Solve Problems

Helps you visualize problems

gets your mind out of your mind's way − Helps to Solve Problems

Talks to your brain the way it understands

− Visually Powerful

make connections - this is how the brain works

− Improves Learning & Memory

no organization roadblocks

nothing to do but add content − Overcome Procrastination & Blocks

adding meaningful images, helps your brain recall

It has already been established that mind maps are useful tools when it comes to solving problems. One of the reasons for this is because they allow you to lay all of the elements of that problem out at once. So, you can see all of the separate issues of that problem at once. This gives you a means of visualizing the problem.

Mind maps also allow you to work through a problem. By chipping away at the different parts of the problem you are able to pin point the problems source and therefore what can be done about it. Mind mapping can also help you to come up with creative solutions for a problem that you are having and help you to walk through each of your solutions as well.

Very often, when people are trying to solve a problem, their brain races ahead of the answer that they feel like they might have or that they do have but can't grasp. The just can't express or elaborate on the answer because they can't get it out fast enough. It is kind of like having something on the tip of your tongue, but you just don't know how to say it. What a mind map allows you to do is write down your thoughts and put them into a recognizable form. With all of this information laid out in front of you in a visual way, you are able to find or come up with the solution more rapidly.

Another benefit that you have is that mind mapping allows you to better understand the questions that you are trying to ask. In other words, you are able to ask yourself better questions about what you are trying to solve.

When you are asking better questions, than you are able to better contemplate what the solution to a problem could be.

This can be extremely important, especially when you are trying to contemplate a multi-faceted or more complex type of problem. These types of problems have to be looked at from different angles and it takes time to come up with a solution. A mind map allows you to break apart the various rudiments of a problem, and examine all of the angles of that problem, in a faster and clearer way than by most other means.

The process of building the mind map alone often allows you to come up with the solution to a problem. If this doesn't work, having everything written out will help you to examine the problem from different angles. Once you are able to examine all the different facets to a problem, the solution usually presents itself.

Mind Maps are Visually Powerful

The brain is a wonderful machine, and it can used in a predictable fashion. Mind maps "talk" to your brain in an understandable way. What that means is because the content includes both visual elements and written text, you are blending at least two types of information together. The brain responds well to new and unique forms of information. Since mind maps utilize a mixture of different images, text, colors, and basic shapes the brain becomes more receptive. The fact that the information is clearly represented through relationships and is well organized also helps it to become more received. Therefore, in combination, these elements are all very powerful.

Mind Maps Improve Learning & Memory

We learn by making connections and associations between things. Mind maps allow us to very quickly and easily associate content, and then we are able to re-associate and manipulate that content to make new things. This is almost like playing with Legos because you can tear them apart and put them back together to form something new. As humans, it is in our nature to learn in this type of manner. This is why children have always loved to play with and manipulate toys like blocks.

This type of problem solving is at the root of what we are. It is the core of how we, as humans, learn to tackle the challenges of our world. From birth we are naturally drawn to this type of play, and throughout our lifetimes such 'play' improves our memory and our ability to reason things out. Mind maps allow you to 'play' in this sort of way.

Overcoming Procrastination & Blocks

Did you know that it has been proven that adults have the ability to learn as quickly as children do? The only reason why adults don't take in information 'like a sponge' in the same way children do is because as we grow up we block ourselves from playing in the same manner, and we fail to make strong associations. We tell ourselves "I am too old for that'" or "I don't have enough time for such nonsense; I have better things to do". Playing is what allows our cognitive minds to grow, and it is only our own attitude which blocks us from continuing to grow.

Mind maps are a 'free form' type of tool. You are allowed, and even encouraged, to put information into the mind map in different ways. This form even allows you to brainstorm 'on the fly' if you would like to do it that way. There are no limits, really. Everything that you want to do is allowed. Think of it as though you are an artist. You have the freedom to take different concepts and arrange them in any way that you wish. Just like an artist, all you essentially are doing is adding content, and then revisiting that content to make sure that it is arranged into what you want the final product to be. Even then you are simply adding more content until you get it right.

As you add content you allow your mind map to grow. This is not unlike how a tree would grow. In fact, some people prefer to look at mind maps in this way. They see the central point as the trunk, the main topics are the larger branches, and the subtopics are the twigs and leaves. This is yet another example of how you can perceive mind mapping. In any event, you can add as much content to a mind map as you want, as quickly as you want, and in any way that you want. There is nothing to hold you back.

Furthermore, there is no set up involved in creating a mind map. You don't have to preplan, organize, or prepare anything in order to use a mind map. All you have to do is get out a sheet of paper, or in some cases open up a computer program, and start building onto it. There is no requirement for going back and reorganizing the information either, although you may want to if you expect it to make sense to anyone else. You don't have to though. That is the point; you have the freedom to create your mind map in any way that you wish.

Knowing that there is no pressure to create your mind map in a certain amount of time, and no pressure to create them in a certain way, allows you to overcome anything that might cause you to procrastinate. At the very least, you can create the mind map with no pressure involved. Once you begin creating the mind map, however, you will probably find that whatever project you were anxious about doing doesn't seem as bad as you thought.

The part that holds many people up is getting started. However, once any process has begun, it is easy to carry on. Mind maps can open this door for you. They make people feel very liberated, and therefore are able to get started on a project very easily because they know that there are 'no strings attached'.

Mind maps are also great for people with attention disorders, such as Attention Deficit Disorder (ADD) and Attention Deficit Hyperactive Disorder (ADHD). This is because mind maps allow you to write down your ideas as quickly as you like. There is no pressure to organize your ideas right away, if at all, and there is no pressure to stick with it. You can revisit a mind map as many times as you like. Since mind maps allow for so much freedom and creativity, they are easy to stick with, even for people who have shorter attention spans. It is also helpful that you can add as many visual elements to a mind map as you like. In some mind mapping programs, you can even link out to videos and other forms of multimedia if you want to.

There are no limits to what you can do with mind maps. You can add as much content as you want to, as long as it doesn't distract you or others from the mind map's objective. The more fun that you have with your mind maps, the more engaged you will be, and the more you are going to be able to learn or figure out.

Chapter 8

There are an immense amount of things that you can use mind maps for. In fact, there are many more ways to use mind maps than what has been touched upon in previous chapter. Each of the following sections will explain the particular methods involved as well as in what ways it would make sense to use them.

To Do List

When you are mind mapping in order to create a 'to do list', you create a simple outline of what needs to be done. If you want to, you can even create this in a way that it can serve as a check list. You can make this into a PDF for ongoing reasons, or you can also make it into a living document that you add to and subtract from day to day as the things that you need to do change.

As opposed to other types of 'to do lists', this method works better because humans don't really work well with vertical formats. Sure, we are taught to work with this type of format from childhood, but it is not the most optimal method. It is better to be able to categorize information and view it all at once, if possible.

Humans, by nature, have a tendency to skip around the plans we have made. Life often forces us to do so simply because things come up that we are unprepared for. So, we need the ability to be flexible with our plans. Mind maps give us the flexibility to change and reprioritize when we need to.

Not every list is an ordered list. Very often they are made in a bulleted form where there is no particular order involved. This is because we do not like to have things put into any particular order unless we absolutely need to, and most of the time we need the freedom to place tasks where they best fit as we go about our day.

Mind mapping allows you list the things that you need to get done, but in no particular order.

You simply layout the tasks, and you can pick and choose at a glance. On the other hand, mind mapping can better help you prioritize. For example, your central point can be 'Things to Do', and your main topics can include 'Priority 1', 'Priority 2', 'Priority 3', etc. Even in this case you are not locked into accomplishing these tasks in any particular order, however.

Writing

A mind map can be very useful to writers. You can use a mind map to outline each part of the story, making your main points include the 'exposition', 'rising action', 'climax', 'falling action', and 'resolution', and your subtopics for each one outline the events of each part of the story.

Mind maps can also be of a particular use in non-fiction types of materials, because you can actually build an outline of what topics that you want to write about and what facts you want to provide for each of the topics. In fact, many non-fiction authors begin by writing out their table of contents within a mind map, and then adding in the various facts that they want to include as subtopics in the mind map. Obviously, this would be a very efficient way to write a book or report.

One of the main ways that this is beneficial is that it allows you to see how everything lays out before you even begin the writing process. This way you have a chance to better arrange the order of the topics beforehand. This saves you from having to re-arrange the material once it is written, which can be very difficult. That is, if you even recognize that it all doesn't fit together right.

If you are writing a fictitious story, mind mapping allows you to expand upon your ideas easily. You can pinpoint the areas where the foreshadowing in your story needs to go beforehand, for example. You may even have some images that you want to include in the book, but you are unsure of where to place them. Computerized mind maps are especially good for pre-planning your layout in this way because you can just add these images right into the mind map.

Mind maps are also great to use when you are trying to communicate with editors. It makes it easier for them to provide you with feedback early on in the writing process. Again, this saves you from having to go back and re-write your material over and over.

The key is to keep the information within your mind map compact. This causes you to think about the associations between your content beforehand, and yet continue to be creative as you write. Mind maps can also help you to organize thoughts so that they will be clearer to the reader, preplan where to begin and end the chapters to make them fall together right, and play around with new ideas in a quicker, yet deeper manner.

As well as offering you freedom, mind maps can help you to constrain your writing so that you don't get carried away. This helps you to arrange your material in a well-structured and balanced manner. This way you can makes sure that your chapters carry an equal amount of weight and that the topics are all covered sufficiently but not over-explained, for example.

One of the best things about mind maps is that they allow you to brainstorm viciously, but then revisit and tweak the material later. You don't need to constrain your ideas; you can just let them fly and see what you can come up with. Then, you can go back and arrange the information in a more logical fashion later. Once your ideas are better organized, you can send the material onward to receive feedback.

Would you want to write the entire book in a mind map? This is not recommended, although people have done it before. Certainly a short report could be entirely put together in a mind map. Entire presentations can be made using a mind map as well. In fact, this would be a way to present information in a novel way to people who you are working with.

Research

Mind mapping is helpful in research projects because it allows you to draw connections and associations between the topics. This process makes it easier for you to organize the information in the most optimal order as well as sort the topics according to their importance. Being able to see this information laid out will not only allow you to better arrange the information, but to be more creative in how you present the information as well.

It is also helps because it gives you one central place to keep the information that you find. You can keep your mind map simple by placing the links or the page number to the information that you want to refer to within the mind map. This also helps you to cite your sources later on. In addition to this, mind maps are great for research because they allow you to store the graphs and tables that you need inside of this. This gives you the opportunity to pull from them as you work the rest of the information out.

Brainstorming

When you are brainstorming, you are writing all of your ideas down in the most free-style manner possible. It is not unlike spontaneous prose, where you write what is in your mind onto the paper with no forethought about the structure, organization, or even the value of what you are writing. Whether you are brainstorming with a team or on your own, you don't want to dismiss any ideas because they can all be used as building blocks for what you will be trying to create later on.

Once all of these ideas are captured within the mind map, you can review the information, reorganize it, add to it, and cut away where it makes sense to. You can edit and revise these ideas as a group or individually. If you were brainstorming on your own, you can tweak the information just enough to make it understandable to someone else, and then pass it on to friends and family members to see what they recommend that you do with the information.

Mind mapping makes it easy for you to get your thoughts into written form quickly and without hesitation. It also allows you to 'see the whole' picture, so you are able to come up with better ideas. This type of brainstorming helps you to flow from one idea to the other and provides you with a means of separating your ideas by organizing them in different levels or tiers. In addition, seeing several similar ideas clumped together can inspire entirely new and better ideas. You can combine, recombine, and add to the content to come up with better material over all.

Another benefit of brainstorming with mind maps is that they do appeal to different kinds of people in different ways. So, a mind map is a very good 'place' to come together with other people to share ideas since the ideas produced can be presented in a number of different ways. They make it easy to work as a team to revisit and revise the information as a group.

Studying

Students have used mind maps as a way to take notes for centuries. Nowadays, many students, whether in grade school or college, have the luxury of having a computer sitting right in front of them. If you are a student, it is very easy to pull up some mind mapping software and type in the most critical points of a lecture. You can still, of course, do this on paper if that is easier for you.

If you keep your mind map simple and only write down the essential points, you can spend more time taking in the information audibly and visibly. Later on, you will be able to quickly review your mind map, which will bring back the memory of what was stated by the instructor. Another thing that you can do is get permission from your teacher to make an audio recording of the lesson. This way, you can study the material later on by looking at the mind map and listening to the lecture at the same time.

Taking notes in the manner helps you focus on the central ideas behind the information. You can also break those ideas down, listing the various elements that make up the topic. It also is a very quick and easy way to take notes since you can draw lines and arrows between the information to make clear how they are connected. This also is a socially acceptable way to doodle out images that are representative of the material. You can add or create charts to your mind map as well, which can help you to understand and memorize data.

Reviewing the material shortly after class has been shown to help people retain information much better. The act of building a mind map out of the material being studied will also help you to recall it later on. That is because this is an exercise, and using an exercise while learning material drives it into your mind and makes it vastly more memorable. In other words, the act of doing something with the material that you are learning provides 'landmarks' for your memory to return to and therefore anchors the information in your memory. Finally, using a mind map in combination with your own learning style is going to help you learn and retain information almost effortlessly.

Studying

Planning

Problem Solving

Estimating Project Time

Taking Notes

Teachers

School

Students

Planning

A mind map can be a very helpful device to use for planning just about anything. Whether you are planning a trip to the grocery store or planning how to build a house, mind maps can help you break the process into simple steps. Mapping out the steps that you need to take will help to ensure that you are not leaving anything out. If you have forgotten something, then you can simply add it in to ensure that it gets done. It also allows you to better enjoy the progress as you accomplish these goals and as you are able to remove them from your list or check them off as done.

Do you see how this method can help you to keep track of the progress in a more feasible manner than other checklists could? Creating a mind map before you begin a project also helps you to have an idea of what the outcome ought to be. Furthermore, it helps you to ensure the outcome comes about as planned. Essentially all that you have to do is follow three easy steps: plan, do, check. By following these steps, you can assure that the project is done completely and done right.

It has been well established that mind maps help you to see the relationships between things. This can really save you time and in most cases money. Say, for example, that you are planning on building onto your house. You could list the materials that you need in each of the various stages in the project, along with any prices that you have found online. You can simply hand this info off to your carpenter to ensure that he doesn't spend too much on materials. If it is something that you are doing yourself, this would save you from having to run back and forth to the hardware store.

Problem Solving

If you are having trouble with a specific problem, and you write it out in a mind map and leave it be for a while. This helps you to revisit or relearn the problem. Plus, this will allow the problem to stew in your subconscious mind. Leaving a problem for a while and then coming back to it has been proven to make problems easier to solve.

Mind maps also help you to ask better questions about the problem itself. If you do this correctly, the mind map helps you to break up the most difficult parts of the problem into smaller problems that are easier to understand and easier to solve. From there, you can start asking questions that pertain to these, now smaller, problems. Many people use this type of strategy for solving their problems. Since mind maps are built to break down information, using a mind map makes this process is much simpler and much clearer.

Once you have broken down a problem into many smaller, more manageable problems, you can begin tackling them one by one. You can use the mind map to brainstorm different solutions for each problem if they aren't obvious already. Once you start chipping away at the problem, no matter what it is, it will disappear. At the very least you will know what the very first steps to solving it will be.

Estimating Project Time

The process of using mind maps to better manage your time is very simple to the process of planning your projects out. You do this by brainstorming about the project such as: who is the project for, who is going to be doing the work, and what exactly needs to be done. Any part of the work that needs to be done can be brought in as a subtopic. Once you establish what varies tasks need to be done, you can start breaking these tasks into steps.

Once a project is broken into various tasks, it is not hard to estimate how much time each task would take and therefore how long the project should take. The mind map will allow you to ledger things like who does the work, how much it will cost, how much time it will take, and so on. As established above, this will allow you to plan without leaving anything out. So, there shouldn't be anything left unplanned that could take up even more time.

This is really good for people who are detail-oriented because you can see all of the parts of the project right down to their lowest level. On the other hand, if you have a tendency to look at the big picture, then you should be able to take in the most critical parts at a glance and then dive in deeper if they need to. These types of flexibilities are what make mind maps very powerful to use.

Taking Notes

This subject was touched upon in the 'studying' section. You can take these notes just like you would any other way: in a notebook, on a tablet, the back of your book, or even on your phone. Furthermore, you can take them in any shape or form that is best for you, as quickly as you like, and as detailed as you like.

Many people say that it helps them to remember their course content if they re-write the notes when they get home. You can do this with a mind map too. Simply, scribble down the information as best you can when you are in class or a training session, and then straighten it and re-organize it when you get home. This commits the information to memory once more.

Using mind maps is advantageous because they are so versatile. They allow you to think in a linear fashion, if you like, or to think more creatively. They allow you to group and regroup content. You also have the versatility of using a mixture of picture, text, bullet points, arrows, lines, symbols. In other words, you can make them very graphical or very text-driven. You can even doodle on your mind map if it helps you to retain or understand the information.

This amount of freedom is liberating to people. The most important part, however, is that it is fun. Mind maps allow you to play, and play is the most natural way for humans to learn.

School

Mind maps are great for teachers and great for students. In fact, they should be utilized more, according to many of the world's leading scientists and researchers. Mind maps provide very effective ways to present information, and are equally as impressive when it comes to helping people retain information.

One of the biggest problems people tend to have in school is answering the essay question on their test. It probably wouldn't be such a problem if most people realized that it is easier if they mind map out their answer first. All you have to do on the mind map is write down the answer is as the central point and a few main points to support that answer.

As was outlined above, you can use mind maps for studying, as well as for learning and reviewing what you have learned. Mind maps are great for planning out how to tackle your homework. So, they can help you to be very structured. These are great for planning out creative projects as too. You can get your creative juices flowing by brainstorming on a mind map as well. You could even use a mind map to figure out the best way to deal with the school bully, as long as you don't let him see it.

Most people don't think of it, but mind maps work really well when dealing with mathematics. You can take a very complex mathematical problem and break it down into all of its parts. Then you can even describe and define each one of the parts. This is a great tactic for both teachers and students.

Mind maps are an inexpensive and easy way to make presentations for your class. A lot of times they are even more appealing then PowerPoint presentations because you can get so creative with them. Teachers can even use mind maps to present class plans or seating arrangements.

Mind maps are an effective to use when studying in a group. Again, this is because they appeal to multiple types of people. You could even use a mind map to split up the responsibilities of a class assignment when working in groups, or everyone can go home and create a mind map about the material, and it can be reviewed and combined the next day. All of these ideas would apply, to a certain degree, to learning at a work conference or training session as well.

No matter what standing in life you have, mind maps can make you learn more, accomplish more, and be more successful. You have learned various methods for using mind maps. You can put your own personal twist on any of them.

None of these rules are written in stone. The possibilities of what you can do with mind maps are really endless, and so are the possibilities of what they can do for you. It really just depends on how far you want to take it and how creative you get with them.

Chapter 9

There are some ways to create mind maps that seem very basic and very straightforward. However, when you pull the curtain back, you realize that these bland and boring mind maps are actually really quite shocking in the way that they actually work. Mind maps are actually very liberating, enlightening, and encouraging.

Work.

It is really surprising how many people don't know about mind maps. When you talk to people about mind maps and mind mapping to other people, often the idea is totally brand new to people. In fact, for a lot of people even the idea of capturing and utilizing information is something that they don't generally think about. This isn't just you 'Average Joe' either. Many times people who are quite intelligent don't know what a mind map is.

Make some mind maps on your own, and if they work well for you, share your knowledge with others. Show other people what you have done, why you are creating mind maps, and how they have helped you. By doing this, you will really open the eyes of your peers, managers, bosses, etc. You can really help others out this way, and you should.

In terms of using mind mapping in a work setting, mind mapping can really give you the upper hand. Presenting information through a mind map can show your creativity, your design skills, your presentation skills, and your structuring and organizational skills. You may even be able to provide people with some insight to solving some problem simply by visually representing the problem in a mind map.

Running a meeting.

If you are running a meeting of some kind at your job, try using a mind map instead of a PowerPoint. You can use it as a creative tool, a brainstorming tool, a problem solving tool, or even to just illustrate a point in a new and unique way. People are getting so used to seeing PowerPoint presentations nowadays, that people will likely be very interested in seeing information being presented in a new and creative fashion.

Before the meeting ends, you can distribute copies of your mind map. This will cause people to better remember what the meeting was about, and therefore drive your ideas further. Handing out copies of your mind map may even influence people to add onto it. This will not only encourage participation, but might bring out some very creative and useful ideas that may help you to accomplish your goals.

If you conduct a meeting using a mind map, why not make the meeting more fun and interactive by passing out blank mind maps that people can use while reviewing what you say. Then at the end of the meeting, you can ask for them back and later compile the information. This may help you find new ideas that can help to push your company or business forward, or this could help you solve some of the problems that need to be solved. In any case, you are likely to get something out of it, and it will help to make the meeting more enjoyable.

Job Interview.

One thing that people rarely think of is to use a mind map during a job interview. This makes you appear intelligent and well prepared. You can use a mind map to capture information during the interview or to outline your questions beforehand. You could use this opportunity to express how you often use mind mapping to capture and present information as well as to solve problems. Most interviewers would see you as being very smart, proactive, and structured, which can highly work in your favor.

Writing.

In previous chapters, it was mentioned that mind mapping works very well for writing. Whether it is something as big as a book or as short as an essay, this process works very well. In fact, it is probably the most effective tool to use for writing.

It is almost necessary to use mind maps when you are writing books with cliff hangers or choose-your-adventure style books because you have to set up the key points of the story beforehand. Some authors even use mind maps to readjust and refigure information and create different books over and over again with the same content. Adding endnotes and citing sources inside of your mind map can save you hours of frustrating work later on as well.

Networking.

You can also use mind maps for networking purposes. Mind maps can help you to better communicate with other people. For example, if you were to work out a mind map before making an important phone call, this could allow you to better collaborate with the person on the other end of the line. This may also help you to collaborate with a group, or have a group collaborate together better. Again, mind maps are great to use in group settings because they have a way of drawing people because they are so visual and often creatively made.

Social life.

Another thing that people often don't think of is that they can use mind maps to better their social life. One great example is of a man who was actually was able to map out how different people in his community knew each other and were connected. This started out like a game, but over time he was able to use this insight into people's lives to make himself more likeable, make better use of his connections, and further his business extremely well. You could also use a mind map as though it were a little black book or a business card holder by keeping peoples contact information inside and sorting it by what type of relationship you have with them.

Shopping for gifts.

A mind map works great if you are trying to compile a shopping list or a list of gifts. This especially is a good thing to do around the holiday, particularly if you have a lot of people to buy for. This can help you to keep track of things that you have already bought as well as gift ideas that you have and things that the others have mentioned that they would like to have.

Romantic weekend.

Anyone would be wise to use a mind map to plan a romantic weekend for himself and his partner. Not only would you be able to add the perfect touches to your get away, but your partner would likely be impressed by the care and detail that you put into it. Using a mind map to think things through beforehand could also keep you from running into snags throughout your trip and would probably help you to save money on everything as well.

Planning a wedding.

One of the hardest things people face is planning out weddings, and therefore it is the perfect opportunity to put together a mind map. Probably the best time to use a mind map is when you are creating the guest list. You can refer to this list when you are sending out invitations, to make note of the people who have sent in their RSVP, to arrange seating, and even to send out 'Thank You' cards after the wedding is over. Another great thing to do is use a mind map to research what everything is going to cost. Taking a careful look into the price of everything will likely save you money in the end.

Designing your garden.

If you are into gardening, you probably know how huge of a task this can be. You have to plan for different times of the year, you have to plan out where everything would be optimally placed, you have to buy a great amount of material and find the best prices, etc. You can use a mind map or multiple mind maps to organize your plans and keep adding to or subtracting from them throughout the year.

Life.

Many people miss out on a lot of things that they want in life just because they don't plan properly. Making plans allow you to create your life instead of just going with whatever comes your way. The best way to use mind maps to better plan and accomplish thing in your life is to make a practice of writing out mind maps each and every day. This helps you to keep things in focus and provides you a way to solve problems as things come along. When you do this from day to day, it becomes more and more fun. It offers you a way to relieve your stress and away to daydream about what you want for your life as well as what you want for those around you. Most people who do this will tell you that it is one of the most invaluable things that you can do for your life.

Planning family events.

Many people regret that they did not work harder at spending time with their family. This goes back to the previous statement about creating your life instead of just letting it happen. It is easy to neglect family and forego ways of spending time with them. If your family is a priority to you, then you absolutely should use mind maps to keep focus on building upon your relationships and finding ways to spend time together.

Learning a foreign language.

This is another example of things people rarely think of. If you are trying to or want to learn a foreign language, by all means use a mind map. As previously stated, the act of working through a mind map will help you to remember things better. Plus, with computerized mind maps, you can open up and hide the branches. So, why not use this capability to test yourself by showing the word(s) in English and hiding the other word(s) to see if you can think of them.

You could even branch these out a little further to learn more than one language at once. For example, Italian is very close to Spanish; so, by reviewing both sets of vocabulary word at once, you are likely to pick up both languages very quickly. You can even add pictures to help you make connections and retain the information better.

Planning a budget.

Planning your budget day to day is one of the most important things that you can do for yourself and/or your family. One of the coolest things about mind maps is that if you change them from day to day they become almost like a living document. This will not only help you to keep up with what needs to be paid, but keep track of where your money is going as well.

In many cases people don't realize how many different ways they are throwing away money until they see it written out. With a mind map, you can look at the whole scheme of things all at once. Furthermore, using a mind map to look towards the future is going to help you prioritize for the future and find ways to invest or save. Looking at this often will probably also open your eyes to opportunities that present themselves as well.

This will also help you to share your financial information with those whose business it is to know. For instance, if you keep up with your finances through a mind map, at the end of the month you and your spouse can look over thing together in order to make better plans and put limitations where they may need to go. Also, if you have a financial advisor or book keeper, providing them with a mind map can really help them to understand more about your financial situation. This will save them time and help them to do a better job for you.

Starting a new venture.

Starting a new venture is one of the scariest things that you can do. You shouldn't let this stop you though. A lot of that fear comes from the unknown. If you are using a mind map to jot down your ideas, plan ahead, and work out any problems you may have ahead of time, then everything becomes less scary and your anxieties disappear.

If you are starting a new business, every plan that you make can be carefully mapped out. You can make mind maps in order to brainstorm. You can use mind maps to outline your expenses, your product lists, your business connections, and so on. There are templates that you can model after to help you to plan for your business. There is really no end to the different combinations of mind maps that you can use to keep your business not only under control, but more and more productive.

If you would like to take on something new, you can brainstorm different business ideas and you can record information as you test the market to see which ideas would work best. Once you get all of your ideas in order, you can let trusted friends and family members review what you have found to see what they think. You could even take your mind map with you when you go after a loan to show how feasible your idea is and how likely it is to produce returns.

The great thing about mind mapping is that you get both the practice and the product. You can brainstorm new ideas, work with different variables, and solve problems through the process of creating a mind map. After you finish, you have this wonderful document which clearly defines the outcome of everything that you have worked through and you can refer to it or change it again and again.

Again, the possibilities of planning this way are endless. Hopefully, you will put some of the tactics specified above to use. Please remember that these are recommended ways of using mind maps, but they are not the only options that you have. Try these tactics first, and soon you will be discovering new and creative way to use mind maps effectively on your own.

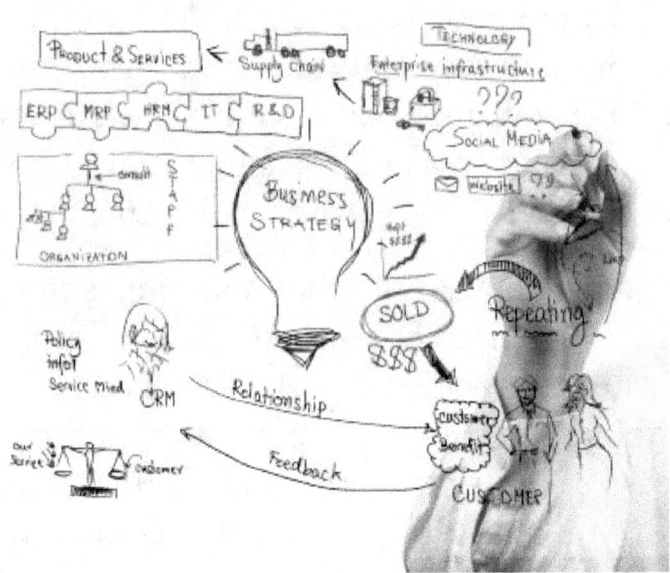

Chapter 10

Mind maps can make your life better. It's as simple as that. They can help you to improve things like the relationships that you have with other people. They can help you to create a vision for your life and give it more purpose. They can help you to create the ideal future that you would like to achieve. You can do all of this by using mind maps for creative problem solving.

By using mind maps you are able to improve your thinking in such a way that allows you to expand your horizons. This allows you to multiply the results of any effort that you put into things. In other words, you are able to have more leverage in the activities that you are engaged in.

You can turn your mind maps into templates to use over and over again. You can use them to better communicate with coworkers and associates. The possible uses for mind maps are just endless, and the sooner that you begin using them in an efficient manner the better things will get for you.

Life Vision and Purpose

There is a mind mapping exercise that you can use to focus more on your life's vision and to give your life more purpose. You can do this no matter how young or old you are, and no matter how rich or poor you are when you start out. Mind mapping is one of the few things in life that you can do to improve your life without investing any money. All you need is a pen and a piece of paper. So, why not allow it to empower your life?

In order to create your life's purpose and vision in the form of a mind map, begin by pulling out a piece of paper and start to think about what makes you the person that you are. Think about your strengths and your weaknesses. When you are doing this, try and put more emphasis on what your strengths are. Also, think about how you think other people perceive you. Now, you want to put more emphasis on your strengths so that you can feel more empowerd. You don't want to think negatively while you are doing this, but you do want to try and achieve the most truthful outlook possible. So, list all of the things that make you who you are.

Next, you want to list all of the things out that really drive you. List all of the things that you are really passionate about. Then, categorize all of those things. After that, make a list of both your good and bad habits.

Also, make a list of all of the things that make you truly happy. In other words, the things that you like to do for yourself, the things that you like to do when it comes to work, activities, and hobbies, and the things that you like to do with and/or for other people. Finally, make a list of things that you would like to get done in the short term, medium term, and long term. Be as specific as possible. You want to get as much of this kind of information captured as you can.

Who do you want to be? What do you want to accomplish? Why do you want to accomplish these things? What are the barriers that are in your way? What is the very next step that you can take for any one of these items that you have written down? What is the very next step that you can take to augment or enhance any of these activities that you enjoy doing? What is the next step that you can take to improve a bad habit that you want to overcome? What can you do to achieve a goal that you've had wanted to meet for a long time? These are questions that you should ask yourself during this exercise.

Maybe you would like to earn a college degree, or maybe you want to get promoted at your job. Specify details like how much that promotion should be for, or the amount of time it would take to earn that degree. Figure out what it would take to accomplish that particular goal. From here you just continue writing and brainstorming these things. The mind map will help you to find the solutions that you need.

Understand that there is no end to a life vision mind map. So, even when you are satisfied with what you have figured out for now, save the mind map because you are going to want to come back to it again and again. As your priorities change, you may want to create a new one. However these mind maps are fluid in their dynamics. Your life vision mind map will never reach an end state. This is an ongoing process.

This vision is very much like the horizon. You will never reach that horizon. If one of your goals is to be a millionaire, for example, you may reach that goal, but you will still be looking to move forward. If you keep previous versions of the mind map, you will be able to look back in time and measure your progress. This can be a very encouraging practice. You really can map out map out the most important things about who you are, and the things that allow you to influence your life and the life of others in positive ways. Doing so will help you achieve and continue achieving the visions that you have for your life.

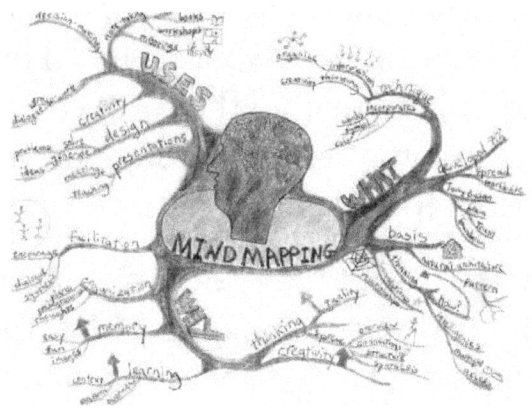

Creating Your Ideal Future

In the previous section you learned how to create a vision for your life. In this section, you are going to learn how to use a mind map to create your ideal future. It is best if this stems from your life vision mind map, but it doesn't have to. You may not ever reach all of the goals that you have to create your ideal future, but you will come a lot closer to it if you have these goals written down than if you don't. In other words, simply identifying what you want will immensely increase your chances of gaining the things you want.

You can begin creating your ideal future by creating a list of things that you really want to get out of your life. This should include things that you would like to accomplish and things that you want to do for other people. You can think about where you want to be in one week, one month, one year, two years, five years, ten years, and even twenty years. You can put all of this into a mind map, and then you can also put steps in place for these things that you want to accomplish in these time frames.

Now, you don't want to be too rigid or too precise, but it is good to map out what the next steps are going to be and try to sort out when you are going to take these steps. You need to think about whom else might be involved in these steps. This is not set in stone, and because it is a mind map you have the opportunity to readjust things as life throws you curve balls and so on. Your priorities may change over time and better opportunities may present themselves. The point is to have a basic outline in place to that will help you to navigate where you want to go.

You want to be positive about all of this. If you put a lot of negativity in your mind map, you are likely to stop yourself short. So, don't set yourself up for failure. Instead, really focus on and insinuate the positive things, the great things, and the strong things. Figure out what you want to accomplish and what it means to you.

Make sure that you specify why you want these things. Tell yourself "I want to do this because..." and then specify the reason. Whatever the reason is, it's going to give you more motivation to achieve these things. For example, saying "I want to save back this much money so that my kids have something left over when I pass on." is going to give you the motivation that you need to take the appropriate steps. Most of us do a lot better when there is a bigger reason than just for our own sake.

Take the time to dream about the things that you want and stay positive as you do. You may not reach the stars, but at least you jumped, right? Don't stress yourself out, just allow yourself to see all the possibilities you can. Again, just having created this list is going to get you a lot further along than just having a dim dream inside your head.

Creative Problem Solving

It has been established that mind maps can help you to problem solve. However, you need to realize just how powerful a tool this can be for you. You now have the ability to blow up every boulder that falls in your path, instead of just working your way around it or breaking it up slowly.

You can do this with any type of problem. It doesn't matter if it is in your work life, personal life, social life, etc. When you have a difficult problem staring you in the face, write down everything that you can think of related to that problem in a mind map. You can do this in a very factual, detail oriented manner, starting from the bottom-up. You can also do this from the top-down, and begin by breaking the problem up into smaller, more feasible parts. If you can, continue breaking these problems down until you find solutions for them.

Just by capturing this information and going through the process of writing these things out, you will feel better about the problem that you are facing. You will find new ways of looking at the problem, and you will find ways to begin working on the problem. Eventually, you will have the problem solved if you just keep focusing on it, or you will be able to come up with the best solution possible. At the very least, you will have a better understanding of what the problem is, even if you can't solve the problem yourself. You will have broken down the problem so well that you will at least know what the next step to take will be and be able to identify who can best help you.

As you can see, mind maps can really make your life better. They can help you to create a beautiful picture. They can help you to understand the future. They can help you to break apart concepts that seem overwhelming or tasks that seem too much to handle. You can use these methods to achieve things that you are passionate about or to create a passion for things that you never even knew that you had. Use them to create the big picture of what you should be and what your life should be. You truly are that powerful, you just need something to help you see the way.

Chapter 11

In this chapter, you are going to be able to learn some advanced tips and tricks. Specifically, this chapter will cover:

- How to make mind maps more appealing

- Creative ways to generate mind maps

- Creative ways to add value to mind maps

- How to model great mind maps

- How to redo mind maps as things change

How to Make Mind Maps More Appealing

You can make mind maps more appealing by adding images and diagrams. In most cases, anything adds to the visual aspects of a mind map is going to make it more appealing. You can find public domain photos, and you can create your own charts and graphs if you are worried about royalty issues. Many mind mapping programs allow you to embed these elements right into the mind map itself. If not, you can always link out to it or out to a webpage that hold the data that you want to share.

You can also do a lot of things to better demonstrate the relationships between topics and subtopics. For example, you can use different colored lines to indicate various types of relationships. You can also use numerous kinds of dots or different dashes within the same mind map to signify different things. In this way you can create and demonstrate different types of connections, which can make your mind map not only more appealing but will allow you to add more data in a very compact way.

These types of strategies are very appealing to people who like to maximize the value of things. There are many other creative ways that you can add extra data into a mind map. Color codes and similar techniques are great for mind maps that need to include a lot of excess information. Color codes can be used to provide better grouping and to generate different ways of thinking about the material without compromising the overall structure of the mind map.

In some programs you can reorganize the content by just clicking and dragging the data. This will give you new ideas and bring out new concepts. You are really creating a new mind map every time you make a new kind of association. Rather than doing this, you can simply use different colors, thicknesses, and symbols so that people can better understand certain association. You can even add legends to your mind map that will let people know what these different colors or symbols stand for.

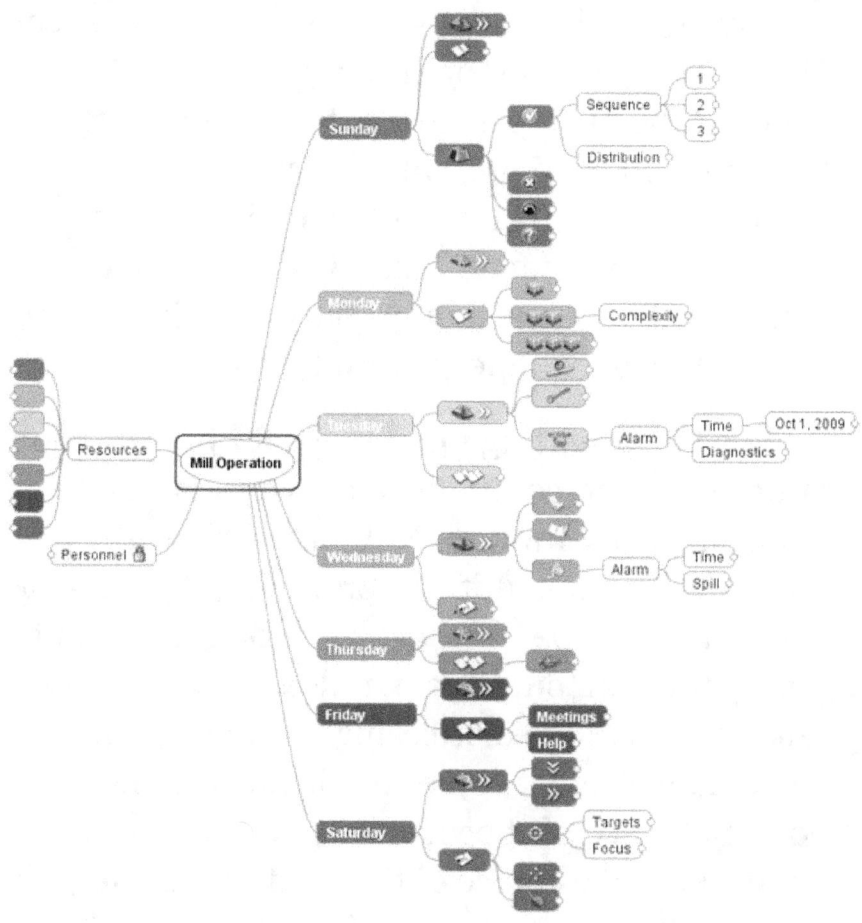

Coding your information in this way is an advanced tactic that you would not likely use in your own personal mind maps, unless of course you wanted to. These tactics are generally used for more complex systems where there is a large amount of data that needs to be demonstrated. They are also more useful when you are trying to communicate complex ideas to others.

Most mind maps can be improved very rapidly by editing and removing content. You have been led to believe that more is better in a mind map, and for the most part that is true. However, when it comes to presentation and communication you want to trim it down to the most needed content. That way it is simple to understand so that it only takes a small amount of time to take in the information.

When you are using mind maps for presentation purposes or to communicate ideas to a number of people, you want to deliberately simplify them. Think about it. If you were given a list of 50 different types of chocolate, you might want to try them all but it's a paradox of choice. Too many choices are distressing to some people, especially when it comes to picking out the optimal piece of chocolate to try. When you are only allowed a choice of three different things, it is simply a much easier decision to make.

When mind maps are chosen to present data, the reason they are usually chosen is because they make it easy to understand complex systems in simple ways. That means that by making your mind map too busy, you are defeating its purpose. Therefore, there are times when keeping a mind map very simple can actually add value to it.

In these types of scenarios, you would want to use simpler and shorter words as well as fewer topics and subtopics. You may even want to add graphs or images that would allow you to eliminate some of the other information. The reason for this is that sometimes too much information can overwhelm or confuse people. By removing and cutting down on data, you are actually adding to the work's clarity.

Creative Ways to Create Mind Maps

It is always better when you can get away from linear thinking and put a little personality into your work. One of the most basic ways that you can get a little creative with your mind maps is to use the symbols that are available. You can get around your usual way of thinking by forcing yourself to think about the content in terms of shapes. For example, you can use circles to signify relationships between different things even though they are in totally different categories.

The better that you are able to frame the content, in terms of connections, the easier you will make it for yourself and others to learn and study the material. If you have a mind map that is circular in nature, all you are allowed to use are main topics with no subtopics at all. This sort of approach forces clarity in thinking. It is a different way to create a mind map. So again, you have a central topic, and you don't allow yourself to come up with anything other than the main topics.

Some mind maps are image based, and in some cases they contain no words whatsoever. For some people, these image based mind maps provide real insight. Imagine a mind map where all of their images are grouped by their dominant color. This would be a great system for teaching children to organize material. For instance, you could have them put the bluest images nearest to the center and the least blue are furthest away. So again, you can use these as learning tools.

Creative Ways to Add Images to Mind Maps

You do not have to be boxed in by what the world sees as a mind map. In other words, you don't have stick with a central node with branches coming off of it. There is no limit to what you can do, and you can get extremely creative if you want to.

There are some really creative ways to use images in mind maps. There are mind maps that are made entirely of photographs. This technique is often used in family tree mind maps and other mind maps used to identify people. For example, you can take pictures and sort the people in them by gender, race, age, or other classifications. You may use this sort of mind map to study stereotyping. You may find that the way people categorize information says a lot about where they were brought up, what their cultural biases are, and even what features they place the most importance on.

You could also start with black and white pictures and then add color in other areas. This would be a very eye catching effect that you can use to make a statement. There are things that you can do to increase the depth of thought within your mind map. Maybe you can increase awareness of poverty in third world countries by arranging pictures of living conditions around the world in a mind map. You could also use black and white photos, sepia, and colored photos to symbolize time or even use brightly colored photos in places on the mind map you want to emphasize and dimmer photos in the less important areas.

Modeling Great Mind Maps

You can usually glimpse at a mind map and tell whether it is professional, whimsical, or personal. You can tell how complex a topic is by looking at the depth of the information. You can also get an idea of how people think. It is fun to watch someone create a mind map and see how they got from 'Point A to Point B' and so on. If you ever get a chance to, try to learn about how they put it together. You might get some insight into new ways of thinking. It is not unlike watching an artist at work.

One interesting thing you can do is look at another person's mind map and then try to create one of your own on the same topic. You will find that yours comes out totally different from theirs. It is likely that you would come up with something different if you tried to create one of your very own over again. If you are writing a book, for example, you could do a different mind map for every single chapter. You can do a different mind map for the same topic again and again, and you will find that you come up with something new every time. This is a great way to come up with more material for your book. You might even think of something that you have never thought of before and that brand new perspective might turn into a new angle for your book. This could work with both fiction and non-fiction topics.

Another thing that you can do is have to two or three people create a mind map on the exact same topic. After they are done you can compare them. This could do a number of things for you. For example, you could get a feel for how your employees think. You can get a feel for different solutions to a problem. You can find different ways to look at products. No matter what the mind map is for, you can get two or three uniquely different perspectives.

Apply these different tips and tricks for your benefit. These are great to use if you are running some kind or campaign or if you are working with some kind of corporation or organization. They can be used when working with a team or in meetings as well. There are creative strategies that you can come up with on your own to use for your personal and professional life as well.

Chapter 12

At this point, you should know why you should be using mind maps, how you should use them, and how powerful they can be. Mind mapping is nothing new, it has been around for a long time, and it has been proven to work. Furthermore, it is an empowering tool that anyone can use no matter how rich or poor they are, no matter their age or station in life.

This is a systematic and methodical tool, yet it gives you the power to be creative as well. It really isn't utilized by enough people. You don't need to be very creative to get creative results. You also don't need to be very smart, yet by utilizing a mind map you can bypass many of the smartest people you know. There are a lot of people who are of an average intelligence, or below average intelligence, yet they use a mind maps and get profound results out of this practice.

In this book you have learned about the various elements that make up a mind map. So, you begin with the central topics, and from there you map out main topics. Afterwards you can branch out to as many subtopics as you like. Each of these topics and subtopics should be related in some way, and through these relations we can come to understand things more clearly.

You can simply scribble out a mind map by hand on a piece of paper, use software to make it, or make an orderly mind map on a piece of poster board to present to others. In actuality, there are no limitations on how to do this. In theory you could make a mind map as tall as the Statue of Liberty, if you had the time, the money, and enough desire to.

You don't have to put a mind map together in the same way each time. Some people do, and some don't. In reality, there are situations when it would make more sense to scribble a mind map out on the back of a napkin at the coffee shop, and there are times when you would really do best to create one on the computer.

Computer mind mapping software is excellent, by the way, and often free. However, you don't have to do it this way. There are times when you will want to just scribble one out really quickly, like when idea hits you all of the sudden. Of course, any ideas that you capture on the run can be added to your collection of computerized mind maps as soon as you have time to input the information.

A mind map and the act of mind mapping are two completely different things. Mind mapping is the act of creating a mind map, and a mind map is the end result of that process. That is if a mind map can even ever really be finished. You can pick up a mind map at any point in time and start mind mapping again. It may also change as you pass it along to others. So, really a mind map is always a living document.

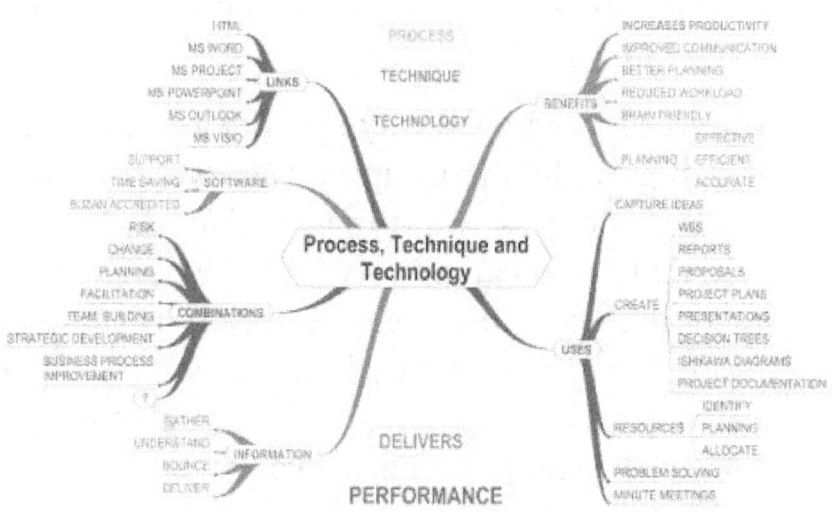

There are some 'right and wrong' ways to use a mind map, officially at least. Mind maps are very visual. The text is part of what makes it visual, but images can be included as well. You can even use multimedia within a computerized type of mind map. You can link out to web pages if you like.

You can create mind maps in many different ways. In fact, the possibilities are endless. They are very much akin to a Swiss army knife, in terms of their versatility. There are many different ways that you can come across the solutions that you want by using a mind map. You wouldn't want to use them for everything though. They are by no means perfect. It is just a matter of understanding what their limitations are and when they are the best things to use and when not.

You were provided a very specific and concise learning method in Chapter 4 that was based on a proven process. Be sure to utilize this information; it can be very beneficial. You were introduced to a number of different learning strategies that were based on this concise learning method. Finally, you were able to devise a learning method of your own.

A lot of information was given on 'learning how to learn'. That is because the learning aspects of mind maps are the most important of all. There is a lot of power in knowledge and the ability to come up with ideas, just ask Einstein, Da Vinci, Edison, and all of the rest of history's greatest people. The more you use mind maps, the more your ability to learn will strengthen.

Mind maps can really be addictive. They are really hard to put down sometimes, particularly when you are finding solutions to getting the things that you want. The creative aspects such as decorating the mind map, finding images, and brainstorming ideas, can be really hard to walk away from too.

You can pan out almost everything that you want to do with a mind map, which really sets you up for success. Some examples of the major benefits of mind mapping are listed below:

- They help you to solve problems

- They help you to organize information

- They help you to communicate with others

- They help you to capture ideas

- They help you see information from different angles

- They help you to learn in a different and robust way

- They help you think in a smarter and more efficient way

There are advantages and disadvantages to using a mind map. It is important that you understand what the disadvantages are so that you can avoid those types of scenarios. For example, sometime mind maps can cause your line of thought to become too simplistic, which does not mix well with certain types of projects. So, if you use them at the wrong time, you are just going to end up confusing yourself and wasting time. Once you start using them on a regular basis, you will most likely be able to recognize when the right or wrong time would be.

Mind maps increase your creativity. This is just a natural part of the process. It forces you to think in brand new ways. Many people get uncomfortable when they are forced into thinking in new ways, but with a mind map it is very comfortable to do so because they carry no pressure. You are simply free to do with it as you wish.

We all learn in different ways. Some of us learn better when we read, some of us learn audibly, and some us are visual learners. No matter which way we take in information, mind maps are useful learning tools to use. One of the best things that you can learn from using a mind map is how to solve problems in creative ways. You will find yourself solving problems in ways that you never even knew were possible.

With a mind map, you are able to learn and memorize content better. That is because they help you to see things in your mind's eye as well as on the page. The process of writing out the content and organizing it helps you to reinforce this knowledge as well. You can play around with the content on a mind map, which also helps to reinforce learning.

Mind maps can help you to become more organized and manage your time better. They help you to overcome other things that block you from becoming successful in life. One of the biggest ways in which they do this is because they provide an easy way to take action, an easy start.

You were offered a number of different ideas on how to use mind maps. There were likely many techniques that you have never thought of before. Hopefully, this will encourage you to begin mind mapping as soon as possible. The ways which were presented were examples of some of the most popular ways. You are not limited to any of these. The ways in which you can use mind maps are only limited by your own creativity.

There were a number of 'shocking' ways to use mind maps that were presented to you as well. These are 'shocking' in that it is really amazing that you can use mind maps for so many different purposes and for so many different reasons, and in each and every case they are still highly effective. Even if you were to use them in the most bizarre ways, they would still likely provide enormous value. The mind mapping process gives you tremendous value, and so does the final result. The actual mind map is often a wonderful artifact that you can use for years to come.

You can never go wrong by at least trying to use a mind map. No matter what you are trying to do, it is a good way to start as a minimum. If nothing else, a mind map is a great crutch. This is especially true when you use a mind map for educational purposes. They can help you to learn very quickly.

Mind maps can make your life better. This statement is absolutely true. You can really plan out significant chunks of your life this way. They are a great tool to utilize for preparing and planning out a better future. They allow you a way to dream up all of the possibilities that you can, along with making it easy for you to move onward with your plans. Furthermore, as time goes on you can always revisit the mind maps that you have created and make any adjustments that you need to.

Mind maps help you to become efficient and make the most of your time. You can continually monitor, plan, and manage the activities that you have mapped out for yourself. By structuring and organizing your life just a little bit better, you will be able to create the life that you want. You can paint the future in such a way that it is visceral and yet tangible. You can create that bottom line of what you want, and you keep your eye on it until it is in your grasp. Along with your own success, you can bring about successes to those around you by sharing what you have learned.

Finally, you have learned a number of advanced tips and tricks in chapter 11. Remember, that you can compress great amounts of information by being creative with your mind map's structure. You also learned that it is both effective and fun to get creative with your mind maps. You can use shading, shadowing, dull colors, vibrant colors, pictures, etc. to add to your mind map's appeal. You can also get creative with the text itself or the elements that you use to link all of the content together. You can even use various graphical elements to show relationships in more than one way.

Mind maps can be extremely powerful tools. There is an endless amount of different methodologies that can be applied to the use of mind maps. You simply have to apply the amount of creativity necessary to achieve the goals that you want. Whether you are a teacher, trainer, educator, student, business person, entrepreneur, soldier, doctor, taxi driver, waiter, and so on, it doesn't matter, mind maps can make a huge difference in your life.

Mind maps allow you to become smarter and more creative, and they allow you to become more successful. This is because they allow you to do things quicker, faster, and in ways that other people rarely think of. Mind maps also allow you to structure information in ways that other people would not be able to do. You truly understand how to put them together and put them to use in your life for maximum value. Most importantly, mind maps allow you to feel empowered and be empowered. This by itself can bring about amazing successes.